Under Two Flags

Under Two Flags

NORMAN G. HISCOX

The Pentland Press
Edinburgh – Cambridge – Durham – USA

First published in 1997 by
The Pentland Press Ltd
1 Hutton Close
South Church
Bishop Auckland
Durham

ISBN 1-85821-497-1

Typeset by Carnegie Publishing, 18 Maynard St, Preston
Printed and bound by Bookcraft Ltd, Bath.

Dedicated to my wife Ethel who for 47 years has put up with the many times when my thoughts and actions have had their origins in those Burma days; also to our sons Derek and Alan. During my writing I have also had in mind our grandchildren, Tom, Hannah, Ellie, Peter and Rachel. To put it simply, I hope they will conclude that in coping with life's ups and downs, God's ways are best.

Acknowledgements

I am grateful to my fellow signallers Dick Williams and Don Turner who figured prominently in my experiences in Burma and India, and whose genuine friendship has continued for more than 50 years. From the time I first mentioned the possibility of memoirs, they marshalled their thoughts and undertook research to enable me to piece together the experiences of those days so long ago. I was happy to include many of their anecdotes. I should say too that without my mother keeping for me so many of the wartime letters which I wrote from the front, I could not have begun to put pen to paper.

Thanks to Alan and Celeste Guerin, Salvationists at Middlesbrough Citadel Corps, for their help with the cover picture.

I appreciate my wife Ethel's diligence in her reading of every page of the draft manuscript and her suggestions for improvement.

I appreciate too the help and encouragement of Mrs Cole and Mrs Denton of the Pentland Press.

Contents

	Acknowledgements	vi
	Foreword	ix
	Introduction	1
1	My parents and the Salvation Army	6
2	A young soldier – SA style	12
3	A soldier – RA style	19
4	A short visit to North Africa	26
5	I convalesce – but not for long	35
6	A longer cruise this time	40
7	From Bombay to Burma	44
8	Preparing for war – it can't be long now	50
9	I meet the Japs	59
10	They shall not pass	65
11	Leave in Calcutta and the SA again	78
12	Back to Burma for the chase to Rangoon	83
13	Approach to the Irrawaddy	88
14	Now for the crossing	94
15	On the road to Mandalay	100
16	Mandalay and the race to Rangoon	105
17	Farewell to 20 Division and back to India	114
18	To the North West Frontier and home	121
19	Awaiting demob – filling in with a bit of acting	126
20	Reflections	130
	Postscript	138

Foreword

One of the very interesting results of the recent commemoration of the Fiftieth Anniversary of the end of the Second World War was the way in which it stirred the memories of everyone who had lived through those six traumatic years from 1939–45.

No memories went deeper or were more traumatic than those of people who had served in the Services – sometimes those memories were so deep and painful that it had taken half a century to be able to face them.

In the case of Norman Hiscox he also writes of his early upbringing with both parents very active in the Salvation Army, which instilled in him a faith which not only carried him through the war but also the difficult post war years. His time serving in the horrendous conditions of the Burma Campaign shows us once more the incredible endurance of young (and older) men transported from safe, ordinary, peacetime lives into the daily horror of jungle warfare, with all the added difficulties of simply staying alive in the terribly hard physical conditions imposed by tropical weather and illness.

The debt we all owe our fighting soldiers in those conditions is invaluable – and to none more than to the Burma Stars of my father's South East Asia Command – of whom he was so very proud.

Mountbatten of Burma

Introduction

THE 50TH ANNIVERSARIES of VE and VJ days in the summer of 1995 meant that, as never before, many ordinary people were able to speak to a wide audience about their experiences in those difficult but challenging days. I am sure that many young people became interested, perhaps for the first time, in how their parents or grandparents coped with life in time of war. What I heard prompted me to shake the dust off all the photographs and letters which I had stored for so long and realise that I too had a story to tell. Like all the other stories, mine is personal and unique to me.

My main interest was in the war against the Japanese as I had spent three years in India and Burma, although before that time I had had a short spell in North Africa. Apart from my own, I had gathered over the years a collection of memorabilia on the conflict. Some were official accounts of the campaigns, like General Slim's *Defeat into Victory*, but others were simply personal stories of soldiers or airmen. I had also kept in touch with two of the 9th Field Regiment Royal Artillery signallers with whom I shared many sticky moments out there, Dick Williams and Don Turner. When I lived in Essex with my wife Ethel and our two sons Derek and Alan, we would frequently exchange visits with Dick and his wife June and family who lived about an hour's drive away. Dick, Don and I would on some occasions meet up in London to attend the annual reunion and concert of the Burma Star Association held in the Royal Albert Hall.

For many years after the war I realised that my time spent in the jungles of Assam, Manipur and Burma, and the habits acquired from rough living, coloured my behaviour to the point where Ethel would say to me after some carelessness in hygiene, 'You're not in Burma now, you know.' Her background as a nurse and midwife, where she had learned meticulous habits of hygiene and cleanliness, contrasted with mine. However, I believe I took her comments in good part and occasionally mended my ways although the phrase sometimes comes out even now. It should be said that my experience also had positive benefits, one small example being that I learned to look after my feet. After all, the comment attributed to Napoleon that an army marches on its stomach is only one side of the coin.

The Burma Star Association has of course lost many members since 1946 but many branches are signing new members. I believe this is because as veterans get to retiring age they begin to reflect more on their time in the forces, whereas in the years after demob most of them wanted to close that chapter and start a new life with a wife and hopefully a family. My own reflections have been about how I coped with the prospect of service life and indeed how my parents managed to come to terms with it, considering that I was the only surviving child of three. I had had a very sheltered and Christian background, my family being active members of the Carlisle Citadel Corps of the Salvation Army. Why didn't I decide to be a conscientious objector or go into the mines as one of my school friends had done? When I think of my upbringing and my very slight physique, I was a very unlikely recruit for the Army; and yet, strange to say, I ended my career as a Sergeant, having spent over three years abroad.

About the time of the VE day celebrations I heard a Chaplain give a short talk on Radio 4 and, in referring to the horrors faced by men in battle, he wanted to remember those who had lost their faith as a result. I thanked God that this had not happened to me although I cannot say how I would have fared if I had been taken prisoner or been severely wounded. Shortly afterwards I came across a library book about Leonard Wilson who was Bishop of Singapore (later Bishop of Birmingham) when the Japanese stormed into the town. He was interned in Changi Jail and questioned under torture for many days to the point that he remained semi-conscious for three weeks. He did not lose faith and said after the war in a BBC

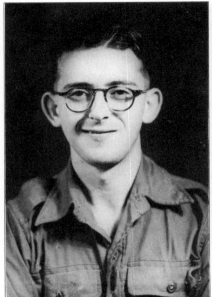

The author and his wife, Ethel.

broadcast that he saw his torturers 'not as they were, not as they had been, but as they were capable of becoming, redeemed by the power of Christ; and I knew it was only common sense to say "forgive".' He arranged for evangelical work amongst the Japanese who had then surrendered, following the dropping of the atom bombs on Hiroshima and Nagasaki, and in 1947 returned to the Cathedral to take services of baptism and confirmation. Amongst those whom he baptised and confirmed was one of the men of the Japanese Military Police who had taken part in his torturing.

Leonard Wilson's story impressed me and so did that of Janne, a Dutch woman who was able to tell, after being silent for fifty years, that she was one of a group of women in Japanese-occupied Java who were forcibly taken away to a large house for the purpose of establishing a brothel for the officers. They resisted as best they could, but had to suffer indescribable indignities for about four months. In the Channel 4 programme 'Witness' the story was told of how Janne encouraged some of these women to take the difficult step of telling their families, and then the world, of their ordeal and humiliation at the hands of the Japanese. Janne, a devout Roman Catholic, testified that although the Japanese took away her dignity and self respect, and managed to scar her for life, they couldn't take away her faith in God.

The Burma Star Association has held a Reunion in the Royal Albert Hall every year since 1946 and, with the 50th anniversary of VE and VJ days, it was decided that the 49th Reunion on 22 April 1995 should be the final one. Dick, Don and I along with our wives agreed to spend a few days together in London and share in the final Reunion. It was a first-class evening and we were honoured by the presence of the Duke of Edinburgh, who is the Association's patron, and the Countess Mountbatten of Burma. Dame Vera Lynn rounded off a three-hour programme of remembrance and celebration, as she had done nearly every year since 1946.

The 14th Army under General Bill Slim has been dubbed 'The Forgotten Army', and few people are aware that, with the support of the RAF, they inflicted on the Japanese Army their biggest defeat of the war, in holding off the advance into India and then recapturing Burma.

When I returned home after demob my mother handed me a batch of letters which I had written during my stay in the Far East. I will need to rely on them for the details of my story. The story of a boy from an ordinary God-fearing home, who had never been any further than a hundred-mile trip to Blackpool once a year, being plunged into the maelstrom of Army life, which took him halfway round the world. Such a Christian background was not unusual, as most churches were well attended and many parents encouraged their children to attend a Sunday School which provided a good grounding for life as well as a faith in God. So wherever I went I was usually able to find like minded people with whom I could link up. No fewer than nineteen young men and women from the Carlisle Citadel Corps of the Salvation Army joined one of the services, so if that was typical of most churches, I was likely to meet up with a number who would share my faith. It would be unreal therefore not to include anecdotes about the Christian people I rubbed shoulders with in various parts of the UK and abroad.

I hope my story will be an encouragement to my grandchildren and to others of their generation who leave home at eighteen, perhaps with some apprehension, to meet the hazards of the wider world.

CHAPTER I

My parents
and the Salvation Army

MY PARENTS WERE BORN over three hundred miles apart, my father in a small agricultural town in the south and my mother in an industrial town in the north almost on the border with Scotland. They were also born eleven years apart. So how did they ever get the chance to meet and fall in love? In the early years of the century the movement of population was very limited compared with the present day. However with poor employment prospects on the land in rural Somerset, my father no doubt realised, like Norman Tebbit's father, that he would have to 'get on his bike'. Indeed this may not have been uncommon in those days as, out of a family of seven, my father, three brothers and a sister had all moved to the Midlands. My father moved out of Shepton Mallet, Somerset, in 1909, when only sixteen, and stayed with a Mr Spencer in Malvern, Worcestershire. Mr Spencer had a butcher's shop, so it is likely that my father was apprenticed in that trade.

Two years later he moved to South Normanton in Derbyshire and there became interested in the work and message of the Salvation Army. He was soon converted, joined the Corps, and became a Bandsman, taking up the trombone. It seems likely that his father Henry, who was a cooper by trade, and his mother Elizabeth, were involved in the Church and made sure that their children attended Sunday School. I have never discovered why my father was given the name Gaius. Thankfully, he also had a second Christian name, Charles. It is strange too that he was not normally known to his family and friends as Charles, but Gaius or Gay for short. This name was used without any embarrassment or innuendo. How times have changed! I was also christened Gaius after my father, but the name is hardly ever used, I'm glad to say. I wouldn't have minded being called Guy, as perhaps 'Guyus' is a more likely pronunciation. I have often wondered if my father's parents liked the name because they were familiar with the third Epistle of John in the New Testament, which in the New International Version begins:

> The Elder, to my dear friend Gaius, whom I love in the truth. Dear friend I pray that you may enjoy good health and that all may go well with you, even as your soul is getting along well. It gave me great joy to have some brother come and tell about your faithfulness to the truth and how you continue to walk in the truth. I have no greater joy than to hear that my children are walking in the truth.

As I was not born until 1923, I can never remember meeting my grandparents, but I have gathered a little more of the way their children were brought up by one or two postcards his sister sent to my father when he left home to go to Malvern. One of them reads: '*Just a card to let you see I have not forgotten you. I do hope dear that you are getting on all right. Mind you are a good boy and be honest in everything and truthful and be quick in your work. Write me a letter soon.*'

The Salvation Army had come into being in 1878. It had formerly been known as the Christian Mission which the Rev. William Booth and his wife had established in the East End of London in 1865. With a new name, the Army grew rapidly throughout Britain and the empire, to the extent that when William Booth died in 1912, it was working in fifty-eight countries. Many Corps were being opened and people in their hundreds were being converted and becoming members (or soldiers as they were known). The growth had been achieved in spite of considerable opposition from what might be called 'the establishment'. So not only my father but also his brother Percy back in Worcester had become soldiers about the same time. Percy later married a 'Salvation Army lassie', who bore him three sons who have been active in various Corps all their lives. The elder son spent a number of years during the war as an officer, dealing with the needs of servicemen for 'tea and chat' at one of the Red Shield canteens which were very popular with the

My parents about the time of their marriage in 1915

men in many parts of the world. The Army had a slogan at one time: '*Where there's need there's the Army.*'

My mother's upbringing was quite different. She was born in March 1881 in Carlisle to John and Isabella Blake, who were living in a terraced house set in a courtyard and sharing outside toilets. With the development of heavy industry the town was growing and John worked as a labourer in the nearby iron works. Sarah Ann was the youngest of a family of four, one of whom was partially sighted and was employed as a representative for the Cumberland Workshops for the Blind. The Education Act of 1870, which was

hailed as an important landmark in English education, had auth-
orised School Boards to allow children into school without payment
and, if they wished, to insist on their regular attendance. Nevertheless, school life was woefully short for most children and it
wasn't until 1899 that the leaving age was raised from eleven to
twelve. Perhaps the Government were thinking of the challenges
that the new century would bring! Anyway, Sally Blake left school
at the age of thirteen. The basics must have been taught quite well,
however, as she wrote to me every week when I was away from
home, and there wasn't much wrong with her writing, spelling or
composition.

The Salvation Army 'opened fire' (the descriptive phrase they
used) in Carlisle in 1880. There was an old wooden building on
an area of waste ground near the River Eden and this was hired
for their meetings. For some reason it was known as 'the match
box' and crowds flocked to the frequent meetings to hear the fervent
evangelists who had teamed up with General Booth. A Salvation
Army Citadel to seat about eight hundred was later built on a site
adjoining Carlisle Castle and another Corps was opened at the
other end of the town where Sally Blake lived with her parents. It
wasn't long before she joined the ranks of the Army, acquired the
uniform somehow, and became a member of the Songster Brigade
and the Corps Cadet Brigade. This latter group were young and
enthusiastic Salvationists who, as part of their training and commitment, would be engaged in what was called 'pub booming' on
Saturday nights. This exercise involved doing a round of the local
public houses to sell the Army's periodical, the *War Cry*, and where
possible engage the drinkers in conversation about their faith. Many
years later my mother would tell me how in a certain public house
her father would be drinking with his mates from the iron works
and, on seeing her come through the door in Army uniform, would
make sure she left the pub pretty quickly. She said she sometimes
managed to sneak into the pub unnoticed by her father through
another door. When she was in need of a new pair of shoes her
father would say, *'You wear the soles out for the Army, let them give
you a new pair.'*

The Salvation Army Citadel on a site adjoining the Carlisle Castle and looking like an adjunct to it

The training in the Corps Cadets led Sally to feel that God was calling her to full-time work in the Army as an Officer and after a spell when she was tested as a Candidate for Officership she set off for the Training College at Clapton, in London. The course lasted only one year in those days, so in May 1904 she was commissioned as a Lieutenant, and over the next few years Adjutant Hine and Lieutenant Blake were the Corps Officers at Tonbridge, St Peter Port (Guernsey) and Parkstone. Then, after six years' experience, she was promoted to Captain and sent to be in charge of two Corps in Wales, Abergavenny and then Abersychan, before in 1913 being given the rank of Ensign and appointed to the Corps in Warminster, Derbyshire. At that Corps, Charles Gaius Hiscox was a Bandsman in the Trombone Section, but as the Army's rules only permit an Officer to marry another Officer, Ensign Blake resigned her commission in order to marry Charles. So my parents were married in November 1915 and found a house in Sally's home town of Carlisle.

Carlisle Castle

It is worth mentioning here that, from the beginning, the Army looked upon the sexes as equal, both as regards the Commissioned Officers and the Local Officers in each Corps. Over the years two women have served as General of the Army: Evangeline Booth, a daughter of the Founder, and more recently Eva Burrows. The General has responsibility for the work of the Army world-wide and not just in Britain.

This story provides the backdrop to my early life. The Carlisle Citadel Corps became the spiritual home of my parents for the rest of their lives, as it was for me and my wife Ethel, until in the sixties we moved to the Epping Forest area of Essex, where I worked in the Education Department of the Essex County Council.

CHAPTER 2

A young soldier – SA style

WORLD WAR ONE HAD BEEN RAGING for over a year when my parents were married. General Kitchener had relied on volunteers but the terrible slaughter of young men during the first two years proved too much for this system and more men were wanted. For nearly a year Parliament had debated the issue of conscription before deciding in May 1916 that every man between the ages of eighteen and forty had to register for service. On moving to Carlisle my father had got a job in heavy industry and this delayed his call-up, although he expected it in 1918. However, the war moved swiftly to a finish following the British defeat of the Germans at Amiens in September, so he escaped the draft. My mother was also working for the war effort. Because of the need for more artillery shells in 1915, Lloyd George introduced the Munitions of War Act and a factory was built for this purpose at a remote location near Gretna Green some nine miles from Carlisle. My mother was transported there every day to fill shells with cordite.

The boom which followed the end of the war came to a sudden end in the autumn of 1920 and by early 1921 there were two million unemployed, my father being one of them. However, as a result of being frugal during the war years, my parents managed to rent a corner shop which a butcher had vacated and stocked it with groceries and general provisions. My parents both worked hard to make the shop a going concern. It was an 'open all hours' little shop which was typical of the times and just like Ronnie Barker's in the TV comedy of that name. They had obviously taken a huge risk in opening up a shop of this kind where none had existed before, but a well known textile firm had their factory across the

road from the shop and my parents guessed right that much of their trade would come from the workers.

I first saw the light of day in May 1923 in the room above the shop and grew up thinking that I was an only child until I discovered many years later that my parents had buried a little boy in October 1918 and a still-born child in March 1920. I was not aware of their sadness at the loss of two babies, but no doubt their Christian faith helped them to cope. My mother was in her late thirties when she had her first child and immunisation against common childhood diseases had not yet arrived; one in ten children died before the age of five. In fact my mother's sister had a baby who died after two years and sadly she and her husband were not able to have any more children. I vividly recall seeing the large framed photograph of their beautiful little girl, prominently displayed in the living room of my aunt and uncle's home. I don't think I was a sickly child although I was of slight build. In the circumstances I suppose I must had been cosseted by my parents, as I remember hearing that they had sought permission from the Director of Education to let me attend an infants' school about a mile away rather than the one in our area. The reason for this was that they felt I would fare better in a school 'where the children were less rough'. In spite of this, I was not debarred from mixing with the other kids in the street and had a happy childhood playing the games common to the times: marbles in the gutters, cricket in the back lane, and tops and whips on the pavements. In particular, I remember a number of us, still at junior school, gathering around the gas lamp on the street corner in the autumn and even winter evenings, engaging in a bit of horse play or moving off to attempt to play football in the darkened cobbled street. The ball was not a full sized football such as the children use in these days, and it was difficult to see whether your own team or your opponents had possession of the ball at any time. But it all added to the fun. Present day parents wouldn't contemplate such goings on. In the summer we were in our element playing in the grounds of the factory social club which had bowling and putting greens and tennis courts for the workers, but for us youngsters a mini forest of oak and beech trees to climb to our hearts' content. There was a small orchard, too, which meant we could scrump for apples in September.

The Salvation Army played a large part in my life, particularly at week-ends, which were fully given over to meetings both indoors and in the open air, from 6.30 p.m. on Saturday until 9 p.m. on Sunday. As a 'young soldier' there were evening activities in which music and drama were used to the full. For the girls, the Sunbeams and Guards kept them out of mischief. Nowadays they would be called Brownies and Guides. The elder teens had a group called the Legion which under excellent leadership was able to present to packed congregations many excellent stage portrayals of Bible incidents. For the boys, becoming a Young People's Band member and being provided with a brass instrument was a big day, although a few also joined the Young People's Singing Company, maybe with the girls as the main attraction. For me it was the Band, and I have a particular memory of the Band Leader encouraging me, when I was about nine years old, to play a simple cornet solo, a familiar tune of the time to secular words: 'Drink to me only with

35/210 The Carlisle Citadel Young People's Band.

The Young People's Band in 1932. I am seated fourth from the left

thine eyes'. It seemed to go down well with the hearers, perhaps because I was the smallest boy in the Band.

After sitting the 11 Plus examination, I found myself at the Creighton Selective Central School after failing to get to the Carlisle Grammar School. I was consoled by the fact that only about ten per cent of the age group were allocated there, as each year a number of places were made available to fee payers. The Creighton School took about the next hundred boys from the list. The school, along with its sister school, the Margaret Sewell (where my future wife attended), aimed to prepare as many pupils as possible for the Oxford School Certificate, a forerunner of the present GCSE. I managed to get this Certificate at the age of fifteen and stayed on for almost a year to take a secretarial course which was offered to both Creighton and Margaret Sewell pupils. I sometimes think that some credit should go to the Army Recruitment Authorities as my educational standard must have been taken into account in choosing to train me as an Artillery signaller. The work with wireless sets, telephones and morse code suited me quite well and, from my later experience, I thanked God I hadn't been drafted to the Border Regiment which had its Headquarters in Carlisle Castle. Strange to think that the Regiment had a Battalion in my Division in Burma and I was happy to serve with them as an observation post signaller. I learned to respect those lads for their fighting qualities; but more of that later.

At this time I spent most of my spare time at the Army or with friends. I'm glad there was no TV or computer games to keep us indoors in the evenings and in spite of my parents' clear Christian commitment, I was allowed considerable freedom. Of course there wasn't as much cause for parents to be concerned about their children as there is in the nineties. I was a keen table tennis player and I remember spending many hours with my fellow cornetist Hargreaves Johnstone and bass player George Clark at one of the private billiards and table tennis clubs in the town. There wasn't the municipal Youth Club provision that exists now. I dare say it's all taken for granted by today's 'teenagers' (a word not in vogue in those days). Our idols were two Hungarian table tennis players, Barna and Bergman, and I remember visiting the Co-op Hall where they were demonstrating their skills.

I was sixteen when the war broke out and until my call-up papers came two years later was still a cornetist in the YP Band. The Senior Band had sufficient personnel at the time and the YP Band Leader resisted the transfer of his players as long as possible. So we were quite an accomplished group although many were soon to be found in a different uniform in all parts of the world. I'm sad to say that my friend Hargreaves, who had trained as a Sergeant Navigator, was on a bombing mission over Germany when his plane was shot down. He is buried in Bad Muender Cemetery, seventeen miles from Hanover. On the night before his fatal mission, he had attended the Salvation Army Hall in Skegness and the members of his bomber crew had come along with him.

What can I say about my feelings and those of my fellow Salvationists at being asked to take up arms? There was of course the possibility of attesting as a conscientious objector or of opting to go down the mines, as did one of my school friends. I don't remember any discussion on these matters. I believe we were all convinced that evil forces had been unleashed and had to be resisted. I have read that after the war the Bishop of Birmingham, who had been tortured when Singapore fell, spoke in a Church of England Convocation about the historical views of the Christian Church about war. There was the absolute pacifist view, he said, that denied the right of any Christian to take up arms under any circumstances, and there was the view endorsed by the majority of the Churches that there was the right of a nation to defend itself if attacked, or to resort to force in the fulfilment of international obligations. He went on: 'The important thing to notice is that among Christians, pacifists and non-pacifists alike, all have agreed that the claims of Christ are paramount, above and beyond all temporal loyalties, state or country or party.'

Soon after my eighteenth birthday the summons to attend at the Army Medical Centre arrived. I was told that I had passed the medical Grade A1 (who didn't?) and on 15 January 1942 got instructions with a travel warrant to present myself ten days later at the Royal Artillery Signals Training Depot at Bamber Bridge, Preston. The Citadel Corps said farewell to me during the Sunday night meeting. The congregation sang with fervour a song that was used a lot in the war years: 'I must have the Saviour with me for I dare not walk alone . . .' The last verse says:

> I must have the Saviour with me in the onward march of life;
> Through the tempest and the sunshine, through the battle and
> the strife.

In these secular days, no doubt these words would be considered very sentimental, but the Army was keen to encourage its young men and women to 'nail their colours to the mast' as they left home to face temptations of a kind they never knew existed. The Naval, Military and Air Force League Diary which I was given made it clear 'that the rights and privileges of Salvationists serving with HM Forces have been safeguarded in the King's Regulations. The officially recognised index letters for Salvationists are "SA". It is important that they appear in your Pay-Book and on your Identity

Disc.' This same diary also included a text for the year and I have one in my possession now which quotes from Corinthians: 'Quit you like men, be strong'. So when most soldiers were attested as C of E, RC or Methodist, I went off to Preston with SA clearly shown in my pay book and on my identity disc, which of course had to be worn round the neck at all times.

CHAPTER 3

A soldier – RA style

'952941 GUNNER HISCOX, YOU'RE IN SQUAD 108; collect your kit from the Quartermaster and find yourself a bunk in that Nissen hut over there. Parade's at 1400 hours.'

Such was the greeting from the Sergeant as I strolled past the Guard room at the Old Mill, Bamber Bridge. The number 952941 still trips off the tongue more easily than my car registration number, even after fifty-three years.

The winter of 1941/42 was a particularly cold one and certainly the night of Thursday 22 January 1942 was no exception. I heaved myself on to a top bunk, pyjamas on as far as I can remember, greatcoat on top of my three blankets and still I was frozen stiff. That was the last time I wore my pyjamas. For weeks I slept in nearly every bit of clothing I possessed. Why weren't we sleeping in the Mill? It would be a lot warmer. Thankfully the ablutions hut was nearby, except that washing and shaving in cold water in bad light at 6.30 in the morning would take a bit of practice. I expect we'll be free at the week-end, I thought, although I heard a rumour that we would be 'confined to Barracks' for ten days. I wonder what the Salvation Army Corps in Preston is like? Could there be another Salvationist in Squad 108? There's only twenty-one in the Squad so I suppose it's unlikely. Anybody else from Carlisle? These and many other questions were soon answered when we paraded under Sergeant Whatsisname. As we lined up in Regimental fashion with the tallest in the centre and the smallest on the end, I discovered that I was next to Gunner Richardson who like me was not much over five foot, and he was from Carlisle. Further along the line was Gunner Jones, yes, a Salvationist from Liverpool Walton Corps. So I began to feel a little more at home.

The Sergeant seemed quite human, not as was often portrayed in songs and ditties, but then, I reckon we were a fairly easy lot to deal with. In fact the motley collection of civilians who were now Squad 108 seemed after a week to be knitting together and enjoying each other's company. The discipline of the parade ground was doing its work. The Sergeant seemed to be a jack of all trades. We were introduced to the Artillery pieces which were *in situ* around the perimeter, and had some practice at stripping down a Bren gun. Then at last we got inside the Old Mill for classes in Artillery signalling. The programme included the operation of the wireless sets numbers 19 and 22, the technique of telephone line laying, and a look at the First World War signalling favourites, the Aldis lamp and the heliograph. We learned that we would be using these items of equipment, at least the more modern ones, to pass fire orders from the forward observation post to the command post at the gun battery. The fire orders would be in speech or morse code, so we had to get down to learning the code and the procedures for passing messages verbally. In case we were enjoying all these new things too much, a ten mile route march was announced and later on an all night scheme. A day exercise called 'Panda' even took us as far as Carlisle, where we set up a huge wireless mast on the Bitts Park, a place I knew very well, and attempted to get in touch with base at Bamber Bridge. The size of the mast to send signals about ninety miles would be ridiculous nowadays; a lot of progress has been made in communications in the last fifty years.

The first week-end that we were allowed out of barracks, off I went into Preston with Frank Jones to seek out the Citadel Corps. The Bandmaster soon found a cornet for me and a tenor horn for Frank and although for me singing in the Songsters was a new experience, I joined Frank among the tenors and learned to pitch the top line on the bass clef. The Citadel Corps and its lovely people took us and a number of other servicemen and women to their hearts, and for the next six months Frank and I would be off to the Corps at every opportunity. We would usually be invited to someone's home for supper after a meeting or a Band Practice and we would then have to step it out to reach the Guardroom by 23.59

Squad 108 as they 'passed out' in July 1942. I am second from the right in the middle row, Frank Jones third from the left in the front row

hours or we would be 'on a fizzer': the first bit of Army slang I picked up, I think.

About Easter in 1942 I had my first leave at home and was back in the Carlisle Citadel Band, in my khaki uniform this time, to mix with some of the soldiers and airmen from all over the country who were taking the place of the many bandsmen who were scattered far and wide. Our experiences were changing us all very quickly. As for me, I had had no girl friends before I left home, but when given a 48-hour pass in May, my parents agreed that one of the Songsters from Preston could come home with me. Soon however I had to say goodbye to her and the many comrades (again an SA term) who had been very instrumental in easing me into my life in the other Army. I am grateful to God for them – they were doing His work in maintaining the spiritual dimension to my life. Along with those in the Woolwich Corps later on, they provided

– 21 –

happy memories and spiritual resources which I was able to draw upon during my three years in the Far East.

In the second week in July we completed our training and, having all been awarded our signallers badges, we were marshalled for the Squad photograph. I reckon we all made sure that the crossed flags insignia that each of us had sewn on the left sleeve of our battledress was very noticeable to our parents when they received the photograph. Our postings were soon announced and I found out that all but two of the squad were to present themselves to a Field Regiment stationed at Betteshanger near the White Cliffs in Kent. I couldn't believe it. Why couldn't the whole squad be kept together? But the Orders on the board were quite clear: Gunners Affleck and Hiscox were posted to 651 Air Observation Post Squadron, RAF, at Old Sarum Airfield near Salisbury, Wiltshire. 'An AOP Squadron, what was this set-up?' Affleck and I thought. Our training hadn't covered anything to do with the RAF! Once it had sunk in, however, I think we began to believe that we had been favoured, in spite of the fact that we would be losing touch with all our 'muckers' in squad 108.

At Old Sarum we discovered that the Squadron was made up of both RAF and Artillery personnel and that we were joining the first unit of its kind to operate in World War 2. I suppose that was the reason it had not got a mention in our training. There was probably some secret about it. The history of Army flying revealed that men had been observing the battlefield from balloons in the Sudan as far back as 1885 and also in the Boer War at the turn of the century. Then, with the development of aircraft, an Army Air Battalion had been formed in 1911, which led to the formation of the Royal Flying Corps in 1912. A variety of planes had been built for combat in the First World War and the RFC managed to adapt some of these for air observation. The RFC, however, had developed as a support role for the Army, but in 1918 the War Office had concluded that there was scope for an independent arm of the services and so the Royal Air Force came into being. With the possibility of war following the Munich crisis of 1938, approval had been given for the development of a light aircraft which could

Pilot (Artillery Officer) and signaller alongside an Auster Aerial Observation aircraft

operate at low level with enough power and manoeuvrability to survive over the battlefield. It also had to have good visibility to enable the Artillery Officer in the cockpit to see clearly the enemy targets he wanted to attack with high explosive shells. So our new Squadron had been supplied with a suitably adapted single wing aircraft, the Auster Mark 3, and Affleck and I found ourselves in a team of signallers who would be operating our wireless sets tuned in to the Officer in the plane circling above us, ready to pass his fire orders for the gun layers. We rather liked the idea.

The question arose again in my mind: was there another Salvationist in the Squadron? It was a more difficult task this time as the Squadron strength was about a hundred. I visited the Salisbury Corps as soon as I was able but didn't come across anybody I could recognise from Old Sarum. However, I attended one of the Sunday Services taken by the Padre on the airfield and found a soul-mate in Aircraftman Jones, not Frank but Fred Jones this time, who hailed from an Elim Pentecostal Church in Great Barr, Birmingham. Fred and I teamed up for a time but soon 'the grapevine' suggested that it wouldn't be long ,before the Squadron was sent overseas and embarkation leave began to be organised on a rota basis. There seemed to be no purpose in getting involved with the activities of the Salisbury Corps as I had done at Preston and I confined myself to occasional visits on a Sunday morning. My dates for a fortnight's embarkation leave came up and I arrived back in Carlisle with very mixed feelings. I was constantly having to answer the question which all servicemen on leave had to face: 'When are you going back, then?' This question was answered in a variety of ways, sometimes facetiously, 'Oh I've gone AWOL,' and often the answer was truthfully, 'Well, I've only just come.' I think it must have been true for most unmarried lads that fourteen days at home with all your friends gone away began to pall a bit. So I didn't mind returning to Old Sarum in anticipation of the adventure ahead.

The news I got on my return was that the Squadron would board ship on the Clyde, but break its journey on the way to Glasgow at the small airfield at Kidsdale near Whithorn, Wigtownshire, in southern Scotland. In a new position, I suppose the first thing all commanders are trained to do is to make sure a guard is mounted, and obviously there was going to be no exception to this rule even in this 'back of beyond' place. The only thing I remember, then, about Kidsdale was a couple of guard duties in the pitch black of an October night, on the corner of the airfield and dodging the sheep that were no doubt enjoying the luscious green grass. There were no concrete runways at Kidsdale. On those guard duties in that remote spot, however, I learned how it was possible to spend a boring two hours quite profitably. Walking around that perimeter with my rifle slung, I would take my mind back to an Army meeting and sing to myself the familiar songs (we didn't call them hymns in the Army) and then hum one of the marches or other music that I'd played with the band. This tactic not only got me through the two hours, but the words of the songs provided a means of worship and reminded me of the Gospel. There were times in the future when this was also possible in a slit trench in Burma, although often 'the Army meeting had to be closed down' for the sake of giving my undivided attention to the job in hand.

I wish now that I had been more diligent in keeping a diary during those years, but we were discouraged from doing so because of the need for security. On active service the breaking of this rule could have serious consequences. At least I made two entries at that time:

29 October 1942. Set off from Kidsdale via Stranraer and boarded the boat at 5 o'clock. HMS *Circassia*.

30 October 1942. Boat left at 3 p.m., sailed down the Clyde and anchored near Greenock. Passed various aircraft carriers, flying boats etc. Destination unknown.

CHAPTER 4

A short visit to North Africa

THE ADAPTATIONS TO HMS *Circassia* had no doubt been done cheaply and speedily, but when you think of it there was no way that individual bunks could have been squeezed into a ship of moderate size to accommodate the thousands of troops that were to be carried. So bunks were out and hammocks were in, and when it was time to 'hook up' the space was so limited that with the movement of the ship and the many restless sleepers, the scene was like a fairground full of swing-boats. We were accommodated on one of the lower decks and I expect that in normal times with port holes open the ventilation would have been adequate, but with the abnormal number of bodies, you could 'cut the air with a knife' at six in the morning. We were all very happy to be paraded on deck at that hour to get some fresh air, even if we had to run around it about ten times before breakfast. In fact I soon abandoned my hammock and found it was better to curl up in a corner somewhere, especially if it was near a washroom, as I was attacked by sea sickness and, dare I say it, diarrhoea more or less at the same time. I found that I was sharing that washroom with a few other landlubbers in the small hours of the night. It was altogether a miserable introduction to life on a troopship.

Was there anything positive about this introduction to the North Atlantic in early November? Not a lot, although I was learning a few 'dodges'. The washroom figured large in my life for a few days but when I ventured on deck, I remember gazing out in astonishment at the enormous size of the convoy composed of ships of all shapes and sizes. Most of the ships seemed to be peacetime liners, now filled with troops, so what could be going on? I watched the destroyers charging around the heavy seas like sheepdogs keeping their flock in order and was glad I hadn't been called up into the Navy. The pitching and rolling was something to see. There were one or two lighter moments, I remember, as some of our company displayed their musical and acting talents in one of the mess rooms. Until then my musical interests had been limited to Salvation Army Brass Bands and the small collection of gramophone records at home. TV had not arrived in the north and it seemed that at home the radio was largely for news bulletins, plus a regular diet of comedy programmes with Tommy Handley in ITMA at the head of the list. So I was quite thrilled to be introduced to some variety in music; in particular I remember that there was a concert pianist in RAF uniform who staggered me with his dexterity on the keys.

We had still been told nothing about our destination. It was obvious that our course for some days had been due west, to avoid the German U-boats. But after a week our direction was clearly southern and the air on deck was getting just a bit warmer. No tropical kit had been issued, however, so could we be going round the Cape or into the Med? We were aware that if we were going to the Far East then we would be going round the Cape, as the shorter route through the Suez Canal was too dangerous at that time. Rumours abounded and we enjoyed speculating on our fate.

By 5 November we were quite sure that the convoy was heading for the Straits of Gibraltar. Some wag suggested that we could celebrate Guy Fawkes night on the Rock! As we got nearer the Straits other convoys seemed to converge with our own. The speculation was soon ended, however, as we were paraded to be told that we were part of the first combined Anglo-American operation of the war, code-named 'Torch', whose aim was to occupy the whole of French North Africa from Casablanca in Morocco to the Algerian town of Bone on the border of Tunisia. A Western Task Force under General Patton which had come directly from the United States would land in Morocco whilst the Centre Task Force under USA General Fredendall would occupy Oran. We were part of an Eastern Task Force to be landed on the Algerian beaches or, if favourable, at the Port of Algiers itself. The three

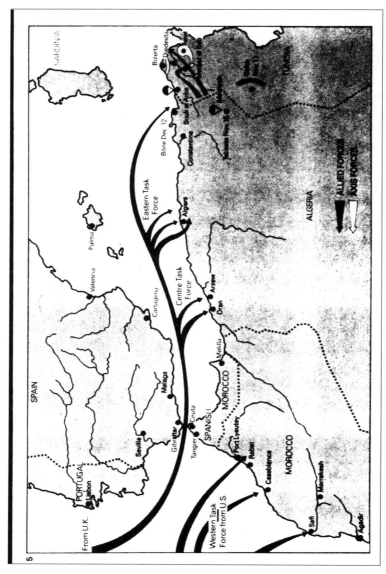

Landings in North Africa

Task Forces consisting of about 600 ships and 100,000 men, British and American, would land simultaneously on the morning of 8 November.

French North Africa was ostensibly loyal to Marshall Petain and there was uncertainty amongst the Allied powers as to how the French troops stationed there would react. However, it proved to be fortunate that Admiral Darlan was visiting the area for purely personal reasons, and he was one of the few men with authority to issue orders which would be obeyed without question. After some hesitation, he lent his authority to the Allies and although there was some slight resistance to the landings at Casablanca and at Algiers, it was soon all over. The Germans were not slow in reacting to counter the Allied landings. Rommel was already being chased out of Libya by the 8th Army following the Battle of Alamein, and he decided to withdraw further into Tunisia to meet the Allied threat from the west. The German High Command also decided to reinforce Rommel's Afrika Korps by landing a contingent from Sicily. On the same day, German troops were landed in northern Tunisia near Bizerta and Tunis, ready to meet the British 1st Army who were quickly moving in that direction from Algiers.

The 651 Air Observation Post Squadron disembarked quite safely at the port of Algiers on 9 November and prepared to move east in support of the British 1st Army under General Anderson. As we gathered our transport together and spent the first night under the trees a few miles outside the town, I experienced my first air raid. The Luftwaffe had also been quick to react to the landings and we decided we had better look for cover. The bombers were going for the port and we didn't seem to be in much danger, but I'm sure the incident reminded us all that we were now in this war for real. We scrambled out of the ditch in a more sober mood, wondering what the next few years would bring. I remember praying in that ditch. I don't quite know what I prayed, something vague, I think, asking God to be with me. I'm sure I wouldn't have been the only one to call on the Almighty; it has been said that there are no atheists in slit trenches. Herbert Davies, a Chaplain in a Far Eastern POW Camp, tells of a Regimental Sergeant Major to whom he talked just before they were taken prisoner by the Japanese. The RSM had then asked, 'Do you really believe all that stuff you spout on Sundays?'

'Yes, of course, or else I wouldn't be here.'

'I can't accept all that – I think it's for women and kids,' said the RSM.

The Chaplain ran into him in the Philippines after the war when they had a chat over a beer. Herbert reminded him of the earlier conversation about belief in God and asked him if he was still of the same mind.

'Padre,' he replied, 'No man could go through the things I've survived and not believe in God.'

The next day our convoy of trucks got underway and camped in the evening in the area of Constantine, about two hundred miles to the east of Algiers. As we camped out for the night, I have a clear recollection of the peace of the star-lit night mingling with the strains of music emanating from one of the tents. I joined the small number in the tent where an officer had brought a few 78 r.p.m. records which he was playing by the light of a single paraffin lamp on a wind-up gramophone. The recordings were largely of popular classical pieces and the music just seemed to match the thoughtful reflections of the men, poised perhaps on the eve of battle. The beautiful and haunting renderings of arias from Puccini's *La Bohème* made an impression on me. I don't think I was familiar with them at the time, but now when I hear 'They call me Mimi' and 'Your tiny hand is frozen' I am transported back to that tent. We made our way through the darkness to our bed spaces realising that it might be some time before we experienced such peace again. Tomorrow we would be in the front line.

The day dawned with an overcast sky and a steady rainfall, but our convoy of lorries formed up with the object, I believe, of joining up with the paratroops who had been landed near the Tunisian border. The Saharan Atlas mountains stretch from Morocco through into Tunisia and the terrain was putting a strain on our heavily loaded trucks as well as on the drivers. Owing to a heavy burst of rain, the winding road had become quite treacherous, and suddenly, to the sound of brakes screeching, I found myself in a heap at the other end of the truck with ammunition and ration boxes on top of me. The truck had skidded and overturned on one of the hairpin bends. How the driver managed to avoid it going over the edge and down the bank I don't know. When I picked myself up, I found that my left arm was quite painful and seemed to be swinging from a point just above the elbow. The humerus bone had been fractured. The others in the truck, including the driver, seemed to have escaped with cuts and bruises, so they were able to arrange for my arm to be put in a makeshift sling and to consult about what was to be done with me. I can't remember much about the next twenty-four hours, except that a jeep took me back down the 250 miles of road to Algiers. At a hospital there – it must have been an Algerian civilian one as the Military had hardly had time to be so organised – my arm was set in plaster and I was fairly comfortable. I was obviously going to be out of action for two or three months and it seemed that I, along with others in the ward, would be on the sideline of Operation Torch. I wondered if I would ever catch up with my mates in the Squadron; the Germans could have been swept into the sea before I could give them a helping hand. I was not to know that I would never see them again. We were astonished to be told the next day that we were to be transferred to a hospital ship berthed in the harbour ready to deal with the early casualties of the campaign. Then, when it was filled up, it would soon be setting sail for England.

The speed of developments was mind boggling. I would have liked to have been able to tell my parents of my accident and that I was on the way home. I don't recall any arrangement for sending letters home at this time and I suppose that was understandable. The last letter I had written to my parents was just before we disembarked at Algiers and, as I discovered later, it did not reach them until five weeks later. In fact they had no word from me for a period of about two months. I have kept a letter which my mother wrote to me on 1 November 1942, addressed to the RAF Station at Kidsdale. It was returned to my mother in August 1943 – yes, ten months later – and the envelope is covered with the names of

Army and RAF field post offices which had been unable to trace me. The last franking of the envelope says 'Field Post Office 8 Aug 43', but they obviously gave up the chase soon afterwards and sent the letter to the RAF Record Office which stamped it 'Return to Sender'. This is what my mother had written:

1 November, 1942

It's Sunday afternoon and I'm writing these few lines hoping you will get it on Monday. I hope my two letters written on Thursday have reached you. We looked for a letter on Saturday and when nothing came we concluded that you had not had time to write, so we may get something tomorrow morning or in the near future. I know you'll write when you can. We were at the meeting this morning, the Officer took it and it was very, very good and the hall was nice and warm which made a lot of difference. Not many Service lads there, we may see more tonight. The Sunday night open-air meetings are finished now as it is too dark. What are you doing with yourself today? I hope you manage to get to a service of some sort with your young friend from the Elim. By the way the allotment book has not come yet, but I'll enquire at the Denton Holme Post Office tomorrow. What do you think of this Training Scheme for Engineering Cadetship? Does it appeal to you? It's all here, read it for yourself. Billy Wilson is going to apply for it and Dad says you might see what can be done about it seeing you have the Certificates and the Credits required. Now I won't say more, this will be a bulky envelope as it is. All our love. God Bless and guide you always.

Mum and Dad

Of course when this letter was being written I was aboard HMS *Circassia* heading for the North Atlantic, but reading the letter again after more than fifty years there is something about the tone which strikes me. Mail was obviously beginning to dry up and although my mother was aware that I was to board ship shortly and must have been concerned about what I was likely to meet, she didn't want to convey any of her anxiety to me. Her encouragement even at that time, that I should consider a future career, suggests a clear faith that I would be returning to take it up. As you would expect, too, she reminded me to seek out a 'service of some sort', a realisation that I could still keep in touch with God and like-minded folks, even if the Salvation Army had to take a back seat for some years. The same thought was very clear to Padre Harry Lannigan during the Battle of Sangro, in Italy. He wrote, 'By this time my war experiences have completely shattered all denominational thinking in me. The war has revealed to me the stupidity of our divisions.' It's a shame that the denominations largely settled back to their old ways after the war, but my experiences may explain why, in recent years, I have been keen to represent my own Church at the meetings of the local Council of Churches.

The hospital ship was much smaller than HMS *Circassia*, the accommodation was good and it had a homely feel to it. The lower decks were laid out in similar fashion to hospital wards. We couldn't have coped with hammocks. As we got under way towards the Straits, it was hard to take in that we were on our own. And as darkness fell, it was an eerie feeling walking round the upper deck festooned with lights, and gazing with some awe at a huge red cross on the forecastle, brilliantly illuminated by floodlights. On the lower decks we found we were free to open or close the portholes at will. So we sailed on and prayed to God that the German U-boat Commanders out there were reasonable men who would respect the Geneva Convention and give us safe passage. But it was nevertheless a bit scary, as we met the big Atlantic all alone and looking like Blackpool illuminations.

As it turned out, we escaped the U-boat menace, but could do nothing to avoid what nature would throw at us. The weather worsened as we ploughed our way northwards, to the extent that when we sat at the long mess tables, some chap who hadn't held on to his bowl of porridge or rice pudding would find that it had slid off the table at the far end. Or if he was lucky it would wing its way back to him as the ship lurched in the opposite direction. So we had to learn not only to hold our food close to our chests but to shift our body weight to compensate for the roll of the ship or we would all have ended up in a heap at the end of the table. The gale lasted for about three or four days and we were told afterwards that it had reached hurricane strength. When we were eventually able to get on the deck, we discovered that most of the lights had been thrown down and a number of lifeboats smashed by the ferocity of the wind. I suppose in hurricane conditions, U-boats have to find the calm of their maximum depth and stay there. It was just as well, as with our diminished lights anything might have happened. However, as December advanced, the Bristol Channel was approaching and we began to think that Christmas at home might be on the cards.

We docked at Avonmouth, and ambulances were ready to take us to Frenchay Hospital in Bristol for a full medical check. We learned that if we were fit enough to travel we would be sent to a hospital as near as possible to our homes. Good thinking by the War Office for a change! So I was given instructions to report to the City General Hospital in Carlisle where I would be issued with the Army blue hospital suit and given treatment to speed up the knitting together of my left humerus bone. It must be realised that in 1942 very few homes had a telephone and as far as I can remember we weren't even given the facility to send a telegram to our parents. Anyway the thought of getting home for Christmas was uppermost in our minds as we collected our travel warrants and wished companions a happy Christmas. I arrived at the hospital in Carlisle and was soon informed that there were strict rules about how many hours patients would be allowed out each day. However, I was lucky enough to be in a downstairs ward near an external door and I saw the possibilities of sneaking out unnoticed. I reckon there was some relaxation of the rules at Christmas time, and it wasn't long before I arrived on the doorstep to greet my astonished parents. Believe it or not, it was Christmas Eve. There was plenty to celebrate the next day.

CHAPTER 5

I convalesce – but not for long

I REMEMBER VERY LITTLE of the two or three months in the City General Hospital except a daily climb up the wall. I mean that as soon as the plaster was removed from my arm, I was taken by the nurse to a suitable section of the cream coloured wall where I was told to stretch my left arm up the wall as far as I could reach. A pencil line marked the high point where my fingers touched, and so the progress made by my bent arm to achieve its normal straightness was plotted on a daily basis. As I describe this process now it seems very elementary and crude and no doubt in 1997 the NHS has developed a more sophisticated method of dealing with fractured limbs which require muscles and tendons to be revived after months of inactivity. But in 1943 there didn't seem to be the pressure to vacate a bed for the next patient to occupy as there is now and in any case I didn't mind staying in Carlisle for as long as possible. On the other hand I was just about climbing up the wall with boredom and after about ten weeks, by which time my arm seemed normal again, I was glad to get rid of the ill-fitting hospital blue and get into my khaki battledress once more.

With all the inactivity over three months, the Army knew I was not fit for more active service, so word came through that I should report to what might nowadays be called a Rehabilitation Centre at Blackburn. For three weeks a Squad of us from many Regiments pounded the roads around Lancashire, threw tree trunks at each other to tone up our arm muscles, and tackled assault courses. You would have thought that the invasion of France was imminent and that we were to be the spearhead. Stalin may have been pushing for the second front to open in that summer of 1943, but it was still a long way off and I couldn't have guessed that a year later, rather than invading Europe, I would play a part in defending India from the invading Japanese. Like most people, I hadn't taken in the full extent of the disasters in the Far East. Since the attack on the American naval base of Pearl Harbour, Hawaii, on 11 December 1941, the Japanese had achieved success after success at sea and on land. Burma, which the Japanese had occupied in 1942, following their rapid success in Malaya, was fleetingly in the news mainly because an odd character named Major General Wingate had led what was called a Long Range Penetration Group through the jungle to attack the Japs in their rear. This group were later to be called the Chindits after the Burmese lion 'Chinthe' which guarded the entrance to the pagodas which are found dotted about all over Burma.

Fred Jones and the rest of my mates in the 651 AOP Squadron with the 1st Army were often in my thoughts and I followed their progress as best I could. The landings along the North African coast had taken the Vichy French, and indeed the Germans, by surprise. But the Germans were building up their forces very rapidly. Two Infantry Divisions and most of the 10th Panzer Division had arrived to help Rommel hold on to Tunisia, so during the early months of 1943 it was tough going for both the British and the US lads. But by the time I was on the move again in May, the German and Italian troops in the whole of North Africa had surrendered or been captured. It seemed that the next push would be for Sicily and the toe of Italy. Taking Italy proved to be a hard slog for the Allies and as far as I can gather my former Squadron did their bit as the 'eyes of the guns' until the Germans surrendered. I've often wondered how different the war would have been for me if that truck hadn't turned over in Algeria.

In the meantime the regime in Blackburn continued to toughen us up and we all wondered where we would be sent next. Perhaps they would post me to a Field Regiment where I might meet up with some of my Preston pals; or another Air Observation Post Squadron? This question could only be answered by the Royal Artillery Depot in Woolwich, South London, to which my next travel warrant was addressed. So the summer of 1943 saw me exploring the capital which as a youngster in remote Cumbria had seemed worlds away. The next couple of months proved to be a worthwhile interlude, full of activity and new experiences.

It was good to join up again with a Salvation Army Corps in the city where the Army was born. I made my way to Whitechapel Road in the East End, where outside the Blind Beggar public house William and Catherine Booth had begun their preaching ministry which developed into the Salvation Army. For thirteen years they had led 'The Christian Mission', until in 1878 the name was changed to The Salvation Army. Apparently it was like putting a lighted match to a barrel of gunpowder. Evangelists became Captains and Lieutenants, members became 'soldiers'. The Army met in 'barracks', the soldiers signed 'Articles of War' and when they died they were 'promoted to Glory'. The Mission Stations also became Corps. Expansion was quick, not only in the British Isles but overseas, so that today the Army flag flies in nearly a hundred countries. The flag (yellow, red and blue) is a symbol of what Salvationists believe. The red centre represents the blood of Jesus which saves from sin, the blue border the holiness which the Christian seeks from God and the yellow star the fire of the Holy Spirit.

In the present day, the man in the street probably looks upon the Army as one of the major charitable organisations and it is true that from the start William Booth linked his preaching of the gospel with the needs of the poor, but the Army's main concern is still, as it was in 1878, a spiritual one. The public appear to have great respect for the Army and generously support the Self Denial Appeal each spring, but I have a feeling that they would consider it to be largely a social welfare organisation, with Christian principles as its motivation. I am afraid that the word 'salvation' may conjure up something quite different from its biblical meaning. Be that as it may, the Corps in Woolwich were very welcoming and at least half a dozen servicemen helped to augment the Band at that time. As at Preston, there were a number of Salvationists who opened up their homes to provide a respite from the austere life in the Barracks. I am grateful to both the Preston and the Woolwich folks for their practical Christianity as well as the guidance in spiritual matters which involvement with them provided.

I took the chance to visit the West End and became acquainted with the historic sights, as there appeared to be a lull in the German bombing campaign. I also remember that 'The Valley' was not far up the road from Woolwich, where Charlton Athletic managed to draw many thousands to their matches on a Saturday afternoon. Of course the Royal Artillery Depot at the top of 'Shooter's Hill' was very proud of its history and a full Regimental muster on the massive parade ground was a few notches up from the squad parades on the car park area outside the Old Mill in Bamber Bridge. Guard duties were very formal. We actually stood outside a box rather like those you see on Horse Guards Parade and were expected to shoulder arms in the correct manner and march smartly twenty-five paces to the right and then to the left before standing at ease in front of the sentry box. A spell of spit and polish did no harm, but it bore little relation to real soldiering on the other side of the ocean.

We were obviously waiting for a draft to provide reinforcements for some theatre of war, but in the meantime, to keep us busy, we would be marched down Shooter's Hill to the Woolwich Arsenal to assist the workers there who were humping war supplies around. We were able to get some idea of how things were 'at the sharp end' as drafts of 8th Army lads from the Western Desert arrived back in the Depot. I remember the tension that was still in their bodies and minds, as they would often walk around in the middle of the night and it seemed that in their sleep they were being transported back to their gun positions in the sand.

But quite soon I was back in Carlisle for another embarkation leave. As with the last one I was too unsettled to enjoy it, although it provided an opportunity for the folks at the Corps to wish me well and assure me of their prayers. Over the next three years I would picture in my mind's eye the Carlisle Corps worshipping God on a Sunday and relive the experience. One other memory of that leave was of going to the Lonsdale Cinema, one of those huge two-tier ones with its organist coming up from the pit, and finding a seat in the circle to see *Gone with the Wind*. Everyone wanted to see this epic, but I found it difficult to concentrate for its four and a half hours, so much so that I came out well before it finished. I think I found the war scenes too much to take at the time.

Back in London it wasn't long before I boarded a packed train to Glasgow and thence to the docks, once more to struggle up the gangplank in full kit for a very long voyage.

CHAPTER 6

A longer cruise this time

T HE WOOLWICH DRAFT was allocated space on the lower deck, much as I expected from my earlier experience of troopships. Clearly the passenger liners converted to troop carriers were only meant to provide a bare minimum of comfort for the other ranks. I believe the officers had some cabin accommodation, on the upper decks away from the prying (and jealous) eyes of the BORs. (This abbreviation for British Other Ranks slipped out as it was used extensively in India to distinguish from IORs – Indian Other Ranks.) Anyway I can imagine that the officers had almost 'cruise conditions', particularly if they belonged to a draft of reinforcements rather than having Regimental responsibilities. I don't remember seeing much of them; the NCOs carried much of the burden of the organisation. However, although the North Atlantic is always unpleasant, things became much more tolerable as we reached the tropics. There was little reason for secrecy this time as we were not an invasion force and when we put into Freetown, Sierra Leone, to take in supplies, tropical kit was the order of the day. About eight degrees north of the Equator, it was exceedingly hot and sticky, a foretaste of what we would experience in India which was obviously to be our destination.

There was an odd duty allocated to us Artillerymen which in a strange way had its compensations. On the stern of the ship there was an ancient artillery piece, so its presence was no doubt the reason for choosing gunners to mount a guard in that particular spot. We were not trained to use the gun, and I doubt if it was in a condition to be fired, so I'm not clear why our presence was needed there. Perhaps it was just to keep us occupied, or maybe it was thought that we would see something that even the Captain couldn't see and provide an early warning of trouble. However, I remember those two-hour duties, often in the middle of the night, watching the ship's wake, the spray sparkling in the moonlight and the silence disturbed only by the swish of the waves around the stern of the ship. Then as we reached the southern hemisphere the Southern Cross appeared in the night sky to remind us how far we were from home. It all seemed so unreal, this scene of beauty and serenity, and yet all around were the destroyers to protect us from a hidden enemy. In a strange way I began to cherish the time spent in that gun emplacement alone with my thoughts. The effect of the brilliant moon was quite magical, and I was somehow brought closer to my parents and to my newly found friends back in the UK.

These reveries came to an end as we rounded the Cape of Good Hope close enough to get a good look at Table Mountain. Then it was only a couple of days sailing to reach Durban. Here we were moved by the welcome given to all troopships by the 'Lady in White' standing on the end of the mole, megaphone in her hand as she sang familiar patriotic songs in her beautiful soprano voice. The war-time mission of Perla Siedle Gibson was acknowledged in August 1995 by the unveiling of a life-size bronze monument on the exact spot where her songs cheered servicemen entering and leaving the port. The story of her unique efforts began in 1940 when she was helping her mother to run a naval canteen. A convoy was leaving the harbour and a young Irish lad who had been entertained by Perla's family called out to her, 'Give us a song.' Cupping her hands, she sang 'When Irish Eyes are Smiling' . . . and a legend was born. From that moment until VJ day she stood on the end of the mole and sang to every troopship visiting and leaving Durban, her billowing white dress, red straw hat and battered megaphone becoming a symbol of love and compassion for millions of servicemen and women. Perla could empathise with the men and women crowding the deck of the troopships, as she herself had two sons in the forces. It says a lot for her dedication that she insisted on singing even on the day she heard that her elder son had been killed whilst serving with the Black Watch in Italy.

With Perla's welcome and the news that we would have to wait

The 'Lady in White' talking to the troops before 'singing them off' as they left Durban for Bombay

a few weeks for another ship to take us to Bombay, we were beginning to warm to the Army life after all. We couldn't wait to be let loose in the town and have a chance to sample the delights of the beautiful golden beaches along the coast. The Army did us proud. We were put into Claremont Camp a few miles away, spent each morning on some necessary fatigues and on the dot of noon were free to join the locals as they piled on the train bound for Durban. We all needed this break. For me the next leave would be about fourteen months away in Calcutta, a very different set up.

Apart from enjoying the rollers on the Indian Ocean beach, I am reminded of a visit to the Durban Town Hall for a performance of Edward German's comic opera 'Merrie England'. Ironically, one of the songs sung by Queen Elizabeth is 'O peaceful England'. Not in 1943! One of the most well known songs, which Sir Walter Raleigh sings, is 'The English Rose'. What nostalgia for the servicemen in the audience. I was also able to experience the international flavour of the Salvation Army as on a Sunday I mixed with the dark skinned 'soldiers' at the Durban Citadel Corps. The work in South Africa, which included schools and medical centres, had been established around the turn of the century, along with countries in the Far East like India, Korea and Indonesia as well as Australia and New Zealand. I began to realise the enormous enthusiasm and vision which had inspired those early pioneers of my mother's generation. The three weeks went by all too quickly and I sampled yet another troopship for the last leg of the journey to India.

CHAPTER 7

From Bombay to Burma

THE ARABIAN SEA at that time of year was very placid and the atmosphere was warm, so it was a delight to put our blankets on what might be called nowadays the First Class passenger deck, to sleep under the stars. We soon came down to earth, however, as we entered the Port of Bombay, the first city of British India. Bombay was a Portuguese colony until 1661 when it was signed off as part of the dowry of Princess Catherine of Braganza who married King Charles II of England. It thus became Britain's first outright Crown Colony in India. Seven years later the East India Company took it over. This company had been set up in 1600 in the reign of Elizabeth I and for two centuries it traded with the East Indies (now modern South East Asia) and gradually took over more and more of India. In 1858, the British Crown became the new ruler in India and when Queen Victoria was proclaimed Empress of India, it became known as 'The Jewel in the Crown'.

From my fairly brief sight of Bombay, the influence of Gothic and Victorian architecture was very evident: the Taj Mahal Hotel, the Victoria Terminus and, although I didn't get a chance for a visit, the Victoria and Albert Museum. My first impression from the rail of the ship was of the teeming mass of humanity, hustling about with goods perched on their heads or loaded into hand carts or bicycle panniers. Then as we were marshalled on the dock side we had our first encounter with the many beggars whom you can't avoid on the streets of every city in India. It seems that fifty years later nothing seems to have changed as Collins' *Illustrated Guide to Bombay* informs the would be tourist:

> Begging is a fact of life in many countries, but it still comes as a shock to many visitors who encounter it for the first time. In Indian

A 'dhobi-wallah' at the RA Depot in Deolali

towns, especially around the streets where tourists go, begging is an organised profession.

However, no doubt the presence of thousands of servicemen provided better employment prospects for the average Indian. At most Army camps dhobi-wallahs, char-wallahs and shoe-shine boys were plentiful. Such was the case at my first destination, the RA Depot at Deolali about eighty miles north of Bombay in the Western Ghats. Yes, there is a such a place as Deolali and as far as I can understand the name became synonymous in the early days of the Raj with being light-headed, staying out in the mid-day sun or generally being bored out of your mind in 'outpost of Empire'.

It was at Deolali rather than Bombay that I had to come to terms with the persistent begging. To keep us fit there was a daily route march in the programme which usually meant that we were followed by scores of children calling all the time, 'No mama, no papa, baksheesh sahib.' The Deolali camp was quite comfortable with well established bungalows, each with a long verandah where the various wallahs would line up to offer their services. Our charpoys (beds) were comfortable too and the rooms were not overcrowded. I was able to sample the delights of an Indian bazaar and have my first photograph taken in tropical kit to send home. The old style 'Colonial type' topee with which we had been issued was quite unserviceable for where we were going and thankfully was soon discarded. The weather was pleasantly warm in late October, the monsoon having passed over, but it would appear that boredom set in after a couple of weeks in Deolali as is evident from a letter I wrote to my parents in the middle of November from a Reinforcement Camp near Comilla in West Bengal.

> Well here I am again and since last writing I've seen a bit more of India. You'll notice the different address but it will be better if you ignore it and use the address as in my last Airgraph dated 13/11/43. I hope you've got it by now although I know they usually take longer than these air letter cards. As a result of this movement I'm afraid there's a lapse in getting your mail but I hope soon they'll be catching me up and going ahead as usual.

> Like most British soldiers I'm never satisfied I guess. We said we would be glad when we got out of the last place but now we say we wouldn't mind being back. I've come across no other Salvationists in India by the way. There was one on the boat however during the last stage of the journey. I've had plenty of decent chums though we've been separated a lot of late. Well I guess I was never a great drinker of tea but this place has made me one. If anyone mentions 'char' (Hindustani for tea) there's a mad rush. I think the main reason is that you must have liquid to replace all you lose in perspiration not that the char is anything special. I'm

writing this in the YMCA hut here in the camp. Every evening I could in blighty, I used to get out of the camp and was browned off if I couldn't, but here I never think of going out. I've just had a game of table tennis – apart from the table not being flat and the light being bad, it wasn't a bad game!

Will I appreciate England, home and beauty after this war – you bet! Most people at home seem to forget Lord Louis's Army out here being bored to tears. Well, don't you let them.

I'm still keeping well. Hope you are the same. God Bless.

Your loving son

This letter was received by my parents one month and two days later. I probably used the word blighty as it was familiar to me from the song 'Take me back to dear old blighty, put me on the train for London Town . . .' but I have learned since that it is an Anglicised attempt at the Hindustani word for 'home'.

Any suggestion of boredom now disappeared from my vocabulary, as I was told that I had been drafted to F Troop, 28/76 Battery, 9th Field Regiment in the 20th Indian Division who were on the Burmese border at a place called Tamu. Soon I was on my way to join them but discovered that the journey would be long and difficult.

My first staging point was to be Dimapur in Manipur State where the 14th Army had its main base, but to get there was a three day journey. The first couple of days were spent very pleasantly on a river steamer on the Brahmaputra, followed by five hours on a narrow gauge railway from Gauhati, passing through beautiful Assamese tea plantations. The heavily loaded train chugged laboriously up the edge of the Naga Hills to Dimapur and we began to realise that the task of supplying an Army would test the resources and ingenuity of the Service Corps. This was a different India from the heat and smells of Bombay and the dust of the Central Plains. The North East is the country's chief tribal area, with a great number of tribes speaking many different languages. I was soon to become acquainted with one of these tribes, the Nagas, and discovered surprisingly enough that most of them were Christians.

The line of communication from Dimapur and the Army's

forward base at Imphal, a distance of 110 miles through the Naga Hills, was a further headache for the staff officers. Halfway along this road, which was still in parts being hacked out of the mountainside by hundreds of Nagas, was a staging post known as Kohima and my next night was spent there. I little knew that this hilltop retreat with its District Commissioner's bungalow in the centre of the village would be the scene of some of the bitterest fighting of the war when the Japanese surrounded it nine months later. I resumed the perilous journey to Imphal the next day. Perilous is perhaps an understatement. In peace time there was little more than a cart track between Dimapur and Imphal. The hills rose to about 5,000 feet around Kohima and plunged down to the plain at Imphal. Following the retreat from Burma in 1942 it was vital to make this track usable by a modern Army, but even in December 1943 whole sections of it were restricted to one-way traffic on alternate days. As we took to the road we were shocked to see not a few lorries burned out at the bottom of the valleys many hundreds of feet below. A Madrassi transport unit using Chevrolet three-tonners was assigned to this road and it seemed to us that familiarity had bred contempt among the drivers, as they whipped round the hair-pin bends, crashing the gears in the process. I distinctly remember a number of us hanging on to the tailboard ready to jump out to save our skins, and on one occasion we did just that as the driver negotiated a bend on an upward slope, then missed his gear-change and the lorry started to run back. As we spent the next eighteen months on the Burma border there was occasionally the chance of some leave back in Bengal but many refused the offer as they did not want to take the risk of the journey on this road.

However, I eventually got to Imphal in one piece. I remember arriving at a camp there late at night and spending one of my most uncomfortable nights since the days of hammocks on the troopship. We were shown to a long low hut where along each wall was a communal bed made out of lengths of bamboo, which is very plentiful in those parts. About twenty of us were told to make the best of it for the night on this contraption. We all learned by bitter experience that there were better ways of using the bamboo and teak trees in the jungle to get a fairly comfortable night's sleep, but more of that later.

A 9th Field Regiment truck was waiting for some of us the next day and within a couple of hours we were in the Battery wagon-lines at the border village of Tamu, set in the jungle-clad Kabaw Valley. An Artillery Troop is composed of four guns each manned by a Sergeant and four gunners, plus a complement of signallers and range plotters. When I arrived at F Troop I found that a number of signallers had their own dug-out, about six feet down with a covering of teak logs and earth, and I was shown to a space in the corner which became home until our move across the border two months later. I hardly realised it, but in fact it was within a day or so of Christmas.

CHAPTER 8

Preparing for war – it can't be long now

TAMU. I had set foot in Burma – just. At least the name easily slipped off the tongue unlike many other places I would come across. Tananarive was a name I heard my new companions talk about for a few days after I arrived. I learned that they had taken part in what must have been one of the least newsworthy operations of the war, the conquest of Madagascar. The Allies had thought it advisable, because of its strategic position, to eliminate the Vichy French forces occupying the Island and instal Free French or British troops there. There had been some opposition from the Vichy French and the 9th Field Regiment had been involved in the landings and in the eventual occupation of the capital, Tananarive. The administration of the island was formally handed over to the Free French early in 1943 and the Regiment made its way to India.

I had reached Tamu after crossing Shenam Ridge, 5,000 feet high in the jungle-clad Chin Hills and a place I would become familiar with six months later. The winding road drops down to Tamu on the edge of the Kabaw valley, known as Death Valley because of a particularly virulent form of malaria which could strike there. I would soon learn that, as we moved our position from place to place, we would merely be moving to a map reference, rather than to living, breathing towns or villages. I have no knowledge of what Tamu village looked like, or its inhabitants, and the same applies to our next position at Witok and subsequent positions at places around the Chin Hills.

I had to become acquainted with the reasons for our presence in the malaria-ridden Kabaw Valley. Following the Japanese attack on

The 'road' from Imphal over the Shenam pass towards Tamu

Pearl Harbour in December 1941, the Japanese land forces had swept all before them, capturing Singapore and the whole of Malaya; in only three months they had also seized Rangoon in southern Burma. Burma, then a British colony linked administratively to India, was ill-prepared for the Japanese assault and although it had been granted a new constitution a few years earlier, the Japanese were able to recruit a Burma Independence Army which helped them in their advance north. Only two small British Divisions were available for the defence of Burma, a country much bigger than France, and the soldiers were not equipped or trained for the task of halting the rampant Japanese Army which had gained battle experience in fighting the Chinese over many years. After the fall of Rangoon, General Slim, who had fought in the Middle East, was given command of the two battered Divisions which were now called Burma Corps and it was inevitable that his mission was to stage a fighting retreat whilst extricating as many of his troops as possible to hold the Japanese on the borders of India at Imphal. He wrote in his book *Defeat into Victory*:

> On the last day of that 900 mile retreat I stood beside the road and watched the rearguard march into India. All of them, British, Indian, and Gurkha, were gaunt and ragged as scarecrows. Yet as they trudged behind their surviving officers in groups pitifully small, they still carried their arms and kept their ranks, they were still recognisable as fighting units. They might look like scarecrows, but they looked like soldiers too.

So it was that in May 1942, the remnants of Burma Corps reinforced by 4 Corps from India (of which the 9th Field became a part) dug in around the Imphal Plain to defend India from the Japanese. As it happened, with the monsoon breaking early and the very long and difficult supply line which the Japanese had to endure, the two armies settled into positions some miles apart, for many months to come. Because of the success achieved by the Japanese army, a myth had developed that the Japanese soldier was a superman in the jungle and in these conditions was invincible. This myth had to be exploded, and in August 1943 two men were brought together who could do just that. Winston Churchill and President

Roosevelt decided to form a new South-East Asia Command to control forces in Burma, Ceylon (now Sri Lanka), Malaya, the Dutch East Indies, Siam (now Thailand) and Indo-China. Admiral Louis Mountbatten was appointed Supreme Commander and General Bill Slim was brought back from India Command to lead a newly formed 14th Army.

General Slim, who became known affectionately by his troops as Uncle Bill, said that on taking over his command he was confronted by three major anxieties – supply, health and morale. The supply problem can already be gauged by the tortuous route by river and road that I had to take to reach Tamu, which I have already described. Supply by air had therefore to be organised. In relation to health, in 1943 for every man evacuated with wounds there were one hundred and twenty evacuated sick. The annual malaria rate alone was eighty-four per cent per annum of the total strength of the Army. Next to malaria came a high incidence of dysentery, skin diseases and jungle typhus, a peculiarly fatal disease. The sick rate of men evacuated from their units rose to over twelve thousand per day. No wonder that, in describing the withdrawal from Burma, the Chief of Staff said that 'death dripped from every leaf'.

Some of the most brilliant research workers in tropical diseases were brought in, and new techniques, drugs and methods of treatment were introduced. Sulphonamide compounds, penicillin, mepacrine and DDT all appeared just in time. The General acknowledged that without research and its results, the Army would not have survived. So when I arrived in Tamu in late 1943, the very first parade of the Troop the next day was for the distribution of mepacrine tablets. The officers were charged with the strict duty of making sure every man swallowed the quinine-laden 'little yellow horrors' which made us all jaundiced. The problem of maintaining the health of his troops was tackled in many and varied ways by General Slim before he could consider fighting the enemy. This was only one way in which the Far East war differed from the war in Europe.

Based on his long experience of the Army, General Slim sets out in his book how he would raise the fighting spirit of his Army and deal with his third anxiety, morale. I was interested to read his three foundations for good morale, which he set out as spiritual, intellectual and material, in that order of importance. In my opinion the way in which he expands on these foundations and puts them clearly in the context of the British, Indian and African troops under his command is quite masterly. Up to this point the Japanese had had success in nearly everything they had attempted, and the lifting of the morale of the newly established 14th Army was vital. I will try to summarise his conclusions which he set out shortly after he assumed command, as I believe they are worthy of wider dissemination.

MORALE is that intangible force, a state of mind, which will move a group of men to give their last ounce to achieve something they feel is bigger than themselves. To endure it must have three foundations, spiritual (because only spiritual can stand real strain) but also intellectual and material.

Spiritual: There must be a noble object which it is vital to achieve by active and aggressive methods and a man must feel that his part in it matters.

Intellectual: He must be convinced that the object is attainable and that he belongs to an organisation which is efficient and has leaders he can trust so that whatever dangers he may have to meet, his life will not be lightly flung away.

Material: The man must feel that he will get a fair deal from his leaders and be given the best possible equipment and conditions for the task.

Bill Slim went on to say that by using the word 'spiritual' as belief in a cause, not strictly in its religious meaning, the foundation was firm. The religions of the various Indian and Gurkha soldiers in his army:

> can rouse in men a blazing contempt for death, and the Christian religion is above all others a source of enduring courage which is the most valuable of all components of morale. We had the advantage over our enemies that ours was based on real, not false, spiritual

values. If ever an army fought in a just cause we did. We fought for the clean, decent and free things of life . . . We fought only because the powers of evil had attacked these things.

These principles provide an insight into the man and why he was so respected by his soldiers. The thought occurs to me that his style contrasts with General Patton of the USA who had to be reprimanded by his superiors for being physical with a soldier he met on parade in Italy. It contrasts too with the Japanese practice of slapping or kicking subordinates.

Lord Louis Mountbatten, a more charismatic character than Bill Slim, also played a prominent role in the improvement of morale. Both of them toured the forward and rear areas beating out themes like, 'Who started this story of the Jap superman? Intelligent free men can whip him every time.' Within a few weeks of my arrival in Tamu, I found myself transported to a jungle clearing, along with representatives from many other units, to hear Lord Louis who was perched on a conveniently drafted soap box, give us this injection of confidence. I believe Slim and Mountbatten succeeded in their different ways in eliminating the defeatist attitude which was prevalent up to that time. This positive theme was reinforced by news of the daring exploits of the 'Chindits' under Major General Orde Wingate who some months before had crossed the Chindwin River and attacked the Japs in the rear, destroying many bridges, ammunition dumps and the like.

Although F Troop had dug in well and protected its position with barbed wire and defensive slit trenches, there was no immediate threat from the Japanese whose main body was still across the Chindwin River. Patrols from both sides were very active so we couldn't be complacent. However, the comparative peace gave us a chance to get used to the conditions whilst occasionally leaving our camp to practise moving into new positions and being prepared for action. Every few nights three of us would be assigned to a slit trench on the perimeter to organise ourselves into two hours keeping watch interspersed with four hours sleep. We would usually draw lots, hoping for the first shift. Two hours in a slit trench in the middle of the jungle at two in the morning was something to

"Who started this story about the Jap Superman? . . . Intelligent free men can whip him every time." Mountbatten's contact with his troops was direct, personal and characteristic

experience. Each man would have his own thoughts, but for the first few times it was hardly possible to think about anything else but 'Is there anyone out there?' If the moon was up, strange shapes seemed to form in the trees and bushes in the shadow cast by its rays. It was also a very noisy place, animals on the move, the screech of jackals and hyenas, then, as it got nearer dawn, myriads of birds telling us to start the day.

This was a time to get used to the limited and boring rations available for the forward troops. We rarely got fresh meat and usually had to make do with packets of oatmeal biscuits instead of bread. We were kept going on a thing called a soya link and the old standby, bully beef. I give credit to the cooks of F Troop who laboured under camp conditions, and later in pouring rain, to give us something palatable. Tinned milk seemed to be fairly plentiful and I remember enjoying at breakfast a concoction made from crushed biscuits (which we called biscuit burgeoo) which was very acceptable as a porridge. I think we all acquired a sense of humour about our life in the jungle, but the frequency of soya links tested this to the full.

The month or so at Tamu was a very useful period to get to know my fellow gunners in F Troop. In the Artillery the other ranks are technically all gunners, although those with whom I mixed most of the time were of the signalling fraternity. We looked to our signalling Bombardier (the same rank as a full Corporal in an Infantry Regiment) to organise our time between duties in the Command Post or at an Observation Post with the Infantry. Other tasks could entail being a member of a party laying a line to an OP, or simply spending a day maintaining our equipment. We learned to respect our Bombardier Cyril Stafford, not only for his sense of responsibility and fairness in dealing with us, but also for his coolness when things turned rough. We learned, too, the serious difficulties of communications in the jungle. The trees absorbed the wireless signals from our 19 and 22 sets, but as it wasn't always possible to lay cable to an Observation Post, we had to learn to persevere even when the 'static' was deafening. It was a great relief to get a response from our 'Oppo' as we sat there fine tuning the knobs whilst bellowing innumerable times into the microphone, 'Hello Charlie One, Hello Charlie One, Report my signals, Charlie One, over.' The Officer would pace up and down until we could tell him, 'We're though, sir.' The notes I had kept from the training sessions in Preston were as much use to me here as the square bashing in Woolwich. So we grew up rather quickly in Tamu, and in more ways than one.

Towards the end of 1943, the new Supreme Commander along with General Slim and his staff were planning for a series of connected offensives for 1944 and one or two of them involved amphibious landings. But the over-riding priority of the Allies for men and materials was the completion of the war in Europe, and even the charisma and the influence of Mountbatten with Churchill could do little to affect this position. So in the spring of 1944 the objectives had to be whittled down to three: limited advances in the south and the north, but a major push on the central front by 4 Corps of which our 20th Indian Division was a part. We knew none of this detail of course, but from the pep talks of Mountbatten and Slim it was obvious that the stalemate was coming to an end. In addition to this we were given notice to move further into Burma nearer the Chindwin River, where the Infantry Regiments we were supporting were patrolling and having some success when they brushed up against the Japs. As OP signallers we soon got to know some of the men in these Battalions which formed 100 Brigade – 4/10 Gurkhas, 14/13 Frontier Force Rifles and the 2nd Border Regiment. I was particularly glad to be linking up with the 2nd Borders as I expected to find men amongst them from my home town of Carlisle. The prospect of mixing with Gurkhas pleased us signallers too, as they had such a good reputation for their fighting qualities as well as their friendliness and cheerfulness.

So we packed up and moved about twenty miles to a place on the map called Witok. The Battery Commander had chosen a site on the edge of the jungle where our guns could cover the low lying scrub and paddy fields between us and the Chindwin River. This was obviously our first serious gun position and quite soon we were ha-rassing the Japs who were massing a few miles away over the river.

CHAPTER 9

I meet the Japs

On arriving at Witok in February 1944, we were quickly engaged in feverish activity to prepare our position for all round defence. Where the jungle, scrubland or elephant grass encroached on our position it had to be cleared, not with bulldozers as we hadn't any, but by the muscles of dozens of us hacking away with machetes. At the same time another squad would wire the perimeter and insert a *panji* every yard along its length. This was the name for a sharpened piece of bamboo forced into the ground with the point at a convenient height to catch an unsuspecting Japanese in the midriff if he attempted to break into our position. Then the gunners would dig enormous pits to site the 25-pounder guns below ground level whilst the signallers and others got on with the slit trenches. A long slit trench for a latrine was always a priority. We didn't have a Padre allocated solely to F Troop but in a book *Thank you, Padre* which pays tribute to their work with the men, the Rev. John Hunter, Padre with the 51st Highland Division is said to have commented: 'It is difficult to adopt a conventional attitude to the person beside you on a pole above a slit trench . . . in such circumstances, real conversations have a habit of developing.'

The routine of digging down and clearing ground which had been practised around Tamu made us feel more secure and we were then able to think about living 'quarters'. Only the Officers had folding camp beds, but the rest of us soon cottoned on to an idea that would rival them for comfort. We would find branches of trees about three inches in diameter and cut a section about eighteen inches in length in the position of a V at one end. Four such stakes would be driven into the ground and two six-foot pieces

dropped into the V slots so that the whole was rather like a fourposter bed. Then all we had to do was to drape our groundsheet over the sides and tighten it underneath by running telephone wire through the eyelets of the sheet. Hey presto, provided the stakes were well grounded we had a comfortable bed. If we were lucky and had acquired a large tarpaulin sheet, we would construct a wooden frame and tie the tarpaulin over it and so provide a bit of 'home from home'. All of this work took some time but later on when we were frequently on the move we had to make the best of it on the ground or in a truck, though we usually managed to stow away the prepared 'bed sections' for use on another day. Of course, for signallers at OPs with the Borders or Gurkhas there was no such 'luxury' but I remember managing reasonable well with a groundsheet and a blanket, provided the ground was soft enough to gouge out from the earth an area where my hip would fit in. If not then you had to manoeuvre to get your hip bone out of the way somehow, or lie on your back which I never liked to do.

After a week or so, while the strengthening of our defences still went on, some of us were able to pitch in with the Engineers who with the help of elephants were widening the log bridges that spanned the dried up water courses or *chaungs*. Beyond Witok the road was little more than a dirt track and yet it soon had to be capable of taking three-ton lorries and even tanks. Working with elephants was quite something. It was a revelation to see them pushing with their trunks logs of up to a quarter of a ton and then by the skilful use of trunk and tusks dropping them on the exact spot to span a dried up river bed.

'Elephant Bill' was valued highly by General Slim. J.H. Williams had spent most of his life in Burma with his beloved elephants and their *oozies* and the General was quick to realise that in the absence of any mechanical equipment for road and bridge construction, here was a ready made asset that could be put to good use. Teak was very plentiful and its extraction from the forests had been a valuable part of the economy of Burma in pre-war years. So, with the rank of Colonel, Bill found himself inundated with requests by various Commanders for the building, widening or strengthening of log bridges over rivers and *chaungs*. The Japanese advance into Burma had, to say the least, been a source of trouble to his elephants and their devoted *oozies*, some of whom had lost their lives. About this time his elephant strength was down to 147, but as he followed the British troops into Burma in 1945, he recaptured many animals from the retreating Japanese and by the fall of Rangoon had about a thousand in his charge. His two books *Elephant Bill* and *Bandoola* tell the fascinating story of his exploits during this period. It is remarkable that he could write a book of 250 pages on one selected elephant, Bandoola, which it seems was a leader of the elephants with which I was involved at Witok. Elephant Bill's devotion to his elephants, and particularly to Bandoola, is clear from the distress this elephant's death caused him and the efforts he made to try to discover who had put a bullet through its brain.

After a couple of months in the Kabaw Valley I began unconsciously to assess what was really valuable and important in life and how, 'back in civilisation', so much was taken for granted. Real comradeship was developing among F Troop gunners and signallers and a sense of 'mucking in together' to make the best of our lot was evident. Water was not on tap any more and most of the time we were rationed to a water bottle full or about a pint a day, so we had to do a bit of sharing when we wanted an extra 'brew up'. Then we had to discover the art of washing and shaving in little more than a mug full. We appreciated like nothing else when our gun position was near a river and we could indulge ourselves.

At this time the patrols of the Borders and the Gurkhas were gathering intelligence about the Japanese intentions and it became clear that the build-up of forces on the other side of the Chindwin River denoted preparations for an early offensive. In fact documents, diaries, marked maps and even operational orders were snatched from the Japs in bold raids on minor headquarters. Lt. General Scoones, the 4 Corps Commander, with his three Indian Divisions 17th, 20th and 23rd disposed between Imphal and the Chindwin, was also ready to begin a push into Burma. The situation posed a considerable dilemma for General Slim. Some of the back-room boys in the safety of Delhi were suggesting that he should 'throw a couple of Divisions over the Chindwin'. Slim was too old a hand to take them seriously. He was determined to beat the Japanese on ground of his own choosing and decided that this could be accomplished by a tactical withdrawal of 4 Corps to the edge of the Imphal Plain where his own lines of communication were relatively short and the Japanese were extended over many miles of jungle-clad hills. From the intelligence reports, Slim and Scoones knew that the Japanese 15th Army under Lt. General Mutaguchi had three Divisions, an Indian National Army Division and a tank Regiment at his disposal, in all 100,000 men. It seemed that his objective would be first, to capture Imphal, and second, to break through to the Brahmaputra valley in Assam. This would have the object of cutting the Bengal–Assam railway which was the lifeline of the Americans and Chinese on the northern front and capturing the airfields from which war supplies were being sent to China. The Generals expected that they would follow their usual tactics and attempt to get behind both the 17th Division on the Tiddim–Imphal road and us, the 20th Division on the Tamu–Imphal road. At the same time, other Japanese columns amounting to some two Divisions would cross the Chindwin at Homalin to the north of us and make for Imphal along the jungle tracks in the Chin Hills. In addition it was expected that three battalions of Japs would make for Kohima in the Naga Hills and so cut the Imphal–Dimapur road and threaten the main base at Dimapur. I've learned since that General Mutaguchi's Order of the Day to the invasion force read:

> This operation will engage the attention of the whole world and is eagerly awaited by a hundred million of our countrymen. Its success will have a profound effect on the course of the war and may even lead to its conclusion. We must therefore expend every ounce of energy and talent to achieve our purpose.

From early March we could feel the tension rising, and the Battery's War Diary for those days clearly illustrates that the storm is approaching:

11th 0930 F Troop moved to forward position and engaged targets Malu – Htinsin area. 50 rounds per gun expended.

12th 0930 E Troop moved to forward position and engaged targets Arty./R. observation Malu – Htinsin area. 50 rounds per gun expended.

13th 1700 Hostile shelling began – S. Witok area shelled.

14th 1800 Hostile shelling area New Witok. Infantry position attacked by tanks – attacked opened by enemy laying smoke screen across S end of paddy in front of position. Tanks and MT heard moving behind smoke screen. F Troop fired over open sights into the screen – enemy withdrew.

1900 S corner of paddy, enemy attempted to lay another smoke screen but wind blew smoke away. F Troop engaged area, fires observed when darkness fell. Enemy tank heard milling around in paddy throughout the night with apparent engine trouble – no sign of this tank when daylight came,

2300 Infantry position at Witok again attacked by enemy – called for support – Battery engaged on previously registered DF [defensive fire] tasks, corrected by FOO [forward observation officer] – attack unsuccessful and enemy withdrew.

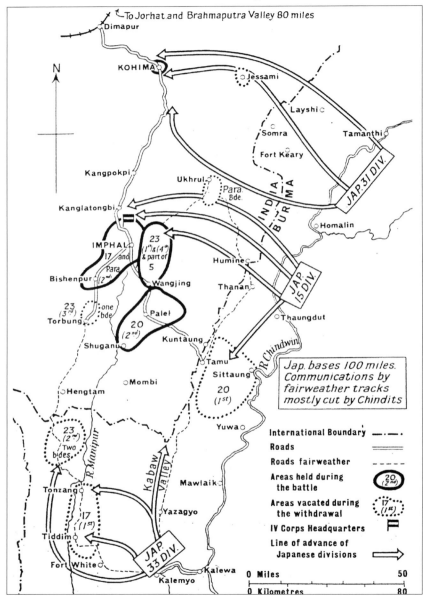

Japanese thrust on Imphal-Kohima

CHAPTER 10

They shall not pass

So the Japanese 'March on Delhi' got under way on the night of 14 March as the War Diary showed and all hell was let loose in the paddy field and jungle clearing around our perimeter. I didn't seem to have a signalling role that night but a couple of us were directed to a slit trench just inside the wire, and warned of an impending attack and to be ready for anything. We soon became aware that the Borders and Gurkhas were engaging what became known as the Yamamoto Force which was spearheading the charge over the Shenam Ridge to reach Imphal within days. The Force had the support of light tanks, which we could hear milling about but could not see how near they were. Very lights or flares were sent up by the Infantry Officers and by the light of them, as far as I could tell, our guns were having a go at the tanks over open sights, which meant they were only a few hundred yards away. All through the night the battle raged 'out there' and the two of us had no other task than to be ready for the Jap if he managed to make it through our perimeter defences. It seemed a very long night stuck in that trench, our rifles at the ready and a few grenades primed for use, and there was no phone to the Command Post to keep us in touch with what was going on. As it was, we kept looking for streaks of light which would herald the dawn and hoped that the enemy had had enough for one night.

Sure enough, with the coming of daylight the Japs dispersed, and we had survived our 'baptism of fire' although one of our cooks had to be treated for shrapnel wounds. Their infantry had failed to reach a position from where they could mount an attack on our defences, which they would have loved to do. We knew that their Commanders were very keen to knock our guns out when they could find them, as they had fewer guns than we had. At one point some of our gunners found themselves rushed by a section of fanatical Japs intent on destroying the guns with pole charges and magnetic mines. The section was lured into an ambush and set around evacuated gun pits and all were killed apart from three who were wounded and turned out to be the first to be captured by the 20th Division. As one of them was an officer, the information he could give was vital to our intelligence. Better still was when a Corporal in the Borders got hold of papers from a staff car which turned out to give details of the strength and dispositions of all the enemy units facing us. The Corporal was awarded the Distinguished Conduct Medal.

During the next few days we were on the highest alert and a pattern was being set which became the norm over the next three months. Being aware of the enemy tactic of attacking at dusk or dawn, we had to be fully prepared at these times, and all of us had to go to our allotted slit trenches ready to meet any threat, even if dawn was as early as half past three. A fifty per cent guard was ordered for the hours of darkness. So every second night after the dusk 'stand to', off we'd go to our favourite slit trench armed with rifle, ammunition, groundsheet and blanket to keep watch over the hours until dawn and 'stand to' again. Memory has faded over fifty years, but I suppose one of us must have had a wrist-watch with a luminous dial so that we would know when to shake our 'mucker' from his slumbers for his two hours' lonely stint. Mind you, the moon over Burma was exceptionally bright and you could almost read by its light. After a few months of this pattern, our idea of heaven was two or three consecutive nights' sleep.

The War Diary shows that on 15 and 16 March 'the Battery engaged targets on call from the 2nd Borders and F Troop fired smoke shells on markers for the RAF to bomb concentrations of Japs to the SW of our position.' The Japs had obviously by-passed us through the jungle in an attempt to block the road to Tamu and cut us off. We were glad to hear that the Borders and the Gurkhas were holding them off. The fighting was heavy and in one skirmish the doctor of the Borders was killed. However, our

Battery Commander Major Morrell had now received the code-word 'Wellington' from the Divisional Commander which was the signal for us to withdraw, so we prepared for the twenty-five mile 'dash' back along the track past Tamu to halt at Moreh. Japanese patrols were active and we had to keep a good look out for them, but it was made more difficult as the track was well rutted and clouds of dust arose as the wheels of the guns and limbers churned it up. However we got to Moreh without incident and hurriedly started our digging-in routine.

We were not allowed to rest, or even get rid of the dust caked on our faces, as the War Diary shows:

19th 1700 Battery in action – Moreh defensive box.

20th 1500 Japanese recce aircraft over position.

21st 1000 E & F Troops registered two targets. Hostile shelling reported.

22nd 0600 Hostile shelling began.

24th 1000 F Troop engaged on targets observed by Air Op.

1700 Enemy aircraft over position, engaged by AA fire.

The Division had delayed the advance of Yamamoto Force by about a week, which doesn't sound much, but the Japanese Commander had gambled on providing his troops with food for only a month, in expectation of them capturing the huge 14th Army dumps at Moreh and Imphal, so they could ill afford any delay. However, we were determined that the Japs should not get their hands on the Moreh dump which, believe it or not, measured two and a half miles by one and a half. It contained a vast supply of food, ammunition and petrol and 32 Brigade and we in 100 Brigade were around to make sure we kept it. Our Divisional Commander knew that the controlled withdrawal to the Imphal Plain involved doing something about this dump, but he felt he had to protest to his Corps Commander that it might be handed over to the Japanese without a fight. However, he was told that the move to pre-planned positions up the hills to the Shenam Saddle overlooking the Imphal Plain had to be executed and so our stay in Moreh was short and sweet. Sweet because our drivers were able to lift from the dump many crates of evaporated and condensed milk and other titbits, before the decision was taken to set fire to it. Some stores had been removed back to Imphal but most of it remained and 32 Brigade had the unenviable task of destroying the whole dump. They slaughtered more than two hundred cattle and destroyed supplies and equipment estimated at one million pounds.

Leaving Moreh and its burning dump behind, 20 Division successfully reached the 5,000 foot high Shenam Saddle, which General Slim thought was the best place to hold off the Japanese approach to the Imphal Plain. The Japanese had chosen this route as their best chance for reaching the Plain and accordingly had reinforced their troops with the object of breaking through at this point. It was made clear to us that the Saddle had to be held at all costs. So when our small troop of guns were found a suitable site on the ridge, the odds were that we would be there for some time. This proved to be the case, as for nearly three months 20 Division clung to various hills and ridges along the Saddle, surrounded by thick jungle, with huge drops to the valleys below. One particular hill came to be known to us as Nippon Hill as the Japs were so well dug in and so determined not to be ousted that they stayed there until the bitter end. They were strafed by Hurricanes, shelled constantly by our guns and attacked by Gurkhas up the slope all without effect. A couple of our guns were sent with the Gurkhas and asked to fire directly into their bunkers from a point halfway up the slope, but when the Infantry went in the Japs were still ready to defend their position.

A number of other hills along the ridge changed hands from time to time, and the nicknames given to them are etched into the minds of all who were there. For some reason the names came from the Mediterranean – Gibraltar, Malta and Crete – but there was also one which we called Scraggy. At that time I reckon the OP signallers and OP Officers must have vied with the Infantry for fitness, as we scrambled up and down those hilltops to provide supporting fire for the 'poor bloody Infantry' who had to deal at close range with the fanatical Japanese whose advance was not going to plan. Bill Slim writes: 'The Infantry, as usual, suffered most, for this was above all an Infantry battle, hand-to-hand, man against man. Our heaviest losses were among the officers, not only in the Infantry, but among the Artillery observation officers, who to give accurate support pushed on with the leading troops.' Thankfully in F Troop, apart from minor problems, we remained unscathed.

It is amazing how human beings can adapt to harsh circumstances when there's really no alternative and they are fully supportive of each other. We just had to make the best of the regular soya links or bully beef, packets of biscuits, little water and often little sleep. When we weren't doing a guard duty at night we had to get used to our guns undertaking a programme of 'harassing fire', that is, a shell or two aimed at irregular intervals at a Jap position for the purpose of disturbing their sleep as well as doing a bit of damage to their bunkers. After a while we found we were able to sleep through this gunfire, probably because we knew it was our own and it was in some way reassuring. But the sound of even a single shot from a rifle was different, and would somehow have us awake and alert for what might be happening. The Japs too had their artillery, although I'm sure that we harassed them more than they harassed us. We called their most common gun a whiz-bang, which was a description of how each shell arrived, without much sound until the very last minute. E Troop at a position nearby caught a whiz-bang or two, but on the ridge F Troop got away with it.

Reflecting on the early months of 1944, I must have been told of the death of my best friend from pre call-up days, Hargreaves Johnstone, who as a Sergeant Navigator on a Lancaster Bomber was shot down over northern Germany on the night of 14 January. Perhaps my parents kept the news from me at the time, as there is no reference to it in the letters to them which I still have in my possession. On the other hand the fighting had really started for me and we regrettably had begun to accept the prospect of hardship, suffering and even death. So it wasn't until after the war that his death really sank in and the Carlisle Citadel held a memorial service for him.

As I've said, 20 Division knew it had to hang on to the Shenam Ridge at all costs, as the Plain with its vast array of supplies as well as the Palel air strip was only a few miles below us to the north. So the motto could well have been 'they shall not pass'. Some of the Infantry encounters have been likened to First World War situations, with the emphasis on close quarter combat, and as gunners we were very keen to give all the support we could to those lads whom as OP signallers we had got to know and respect. Our role was to see that fire was directed on to the Jap bunkers in as large and as accurate concentration as possible, prior to the poor chaps charging up the slopes of these various pimples to take or re-take 'Scraggy', 'Gibraltar' or 'Malta'. Of course we heard of the casualties they suffered and that some of the young reinforcements straight from England had been killed on their first attempt to capture one of these God-forsaken hills. It is not my aim to provide a graphic account of individual encounters which took place on those jungle-clad hilltops, nor indeed could I do so. Such battles have been described vividly in Ken Cooper's book *The Little Men*, the story of a platoon of A Company of the very Borders we were supporting. His book was written in the early seventies, somewhat nearer to the events he described than I am in 1997. However, I am proud to have played my part in making their task a little easier, although God knows ease is hardly a word to use about their lot. Here is a flavour from Ken's book of the life they led: 'The gunners had been called on to "stonk" the Japs for five minutes after midnight. After that I was supposed to walk across no-man's-land and try to grab a Jap. I did not think much of the idea.' At one point in his book Ken also says: 'At about half-hour intervals, 25-pounder guns began harassing the Japs' positions with high explosive salvos, whilst we were digging our trenches. The sound of our guns was comforting.' To us gunners that was good to know.

My letter writing was more spasmodic up on the Ridge, but here's one I managed after I'd had about five weeks to settle up there.

They shall not pass

F Troop 28/76 Battery
9th Field Regt. RA. SEAC
5th May, 1944.

Well, according to the dates it seems 10 or 11 days since I wrote last, but actually it was 2 or 3 days after I got the last letter away. Thanks for Nos. 55 & 56 which have come along since anyway. Yes, it's much better for sleep these days although it's mostly broken into about 3 or 4 hours at a time, what with guard and 'stand to'. I don't think I'm giving secrets away as I've seen it mentioned in print, but there are certain periods, around dawn and dusk mainly, that are most favourable for Japs to attack, so we have to 'stand to' on the alert for these periods. Just now dawn is very early too, so we find ourselves getting hauled up at awful hours. It is only 6 a.m. now and I've settled down to write this letter. That Rest Camp I mentioned is now definitely off for the time being at any rate. There were only about a dozen in the troop who were lucky enough to have 4 days there before things happened. The monsoons are nearly here and as Lord Louis says major operations will almost come to a halt so things may be much quieter and perhaps we can start thinking about rest and leave again.

Let me know who takes over as Bandmaster of the SP&S Band.

O, by the way, you should see what a toff I look now in a bush hat that we've all just been given. You know the kind; a brownish felt hat similar to the Aussies. You may have seen pictures of 14th Army chaps wearing them too.

Glad to say I'm as almost ever fit and well. Time is going on. We've been some time up here now and they don't reckon to keep you very long without relief. Perhaps we'll go out for a break soon; or perhaps we'll keep on wishing.

Cheerio for now and God Bless

I think I must have been too concerned about the censor as the only hint I have given about the Jap attempt to overrun our position at Witok and subsequent withdrawal is the phrase 'before things happened'. Letters home were very personal affairs and I've no idea whether or not I was alone in being 'cagey' about our situation. I suspect most of us were the same, as we wouldn't have wanted to put ourselves at any more risk by a careless word or two. I never heard of anybody being ticked off by the Officers and I don't know how much the blue pencil was used.

There is a first reference in this letter to the *SEAC* newspaper. This was an inspired innovation by Lord Louis soon after he took command. Lieutenant Frank Owen, who had thrown up his job in Fleet Street to enlist, was the Editor and he did a very worthwhile job. The weekly *SEAC* was a great morale booster. It surprises me now that this matter of Eric Ball resigning his Salvation Army Commission ever got into this newspaper. As those who are familiar with Brass Bands will know, Eric Ball went on to be probably one of the most respected and gifted composers of music for Brass Bands in the post-war years. Later in his life he renewed his links with the Salvation Army. Another of the Army's composers wrote a march, 'Under Two Flags', which included strains of 'Rule Britannia' and the national anthem as well as Salvation Army songs, and was written in honour of the many men and women who served under the Union Jack whilst still owing allegiance to the flag of the Salvation Army and its principles. Eric Ball also wrote a song with an appropriate title for the times: 'A prayer for courage'.

The Battery War Diary for 21 May says that F Troop moved to a new position – map reference 572759. The next day was my twenty-first birthday and I spent it in what the diary calls 'digging in and general preparation of the position, defence work and laying of L/T communications'. I don't know whether I even noticed the date.

The 17th Division, who were falling back to the Plain along the road from Tiddim, were also having a rough time as the Japs got behind them to set up road blocks. Additional artillery support was needed and some of our signallers including Dick Williams were sent in that direction. Dick recalls that when he was at an OP the Company Commander of a Gurkha Regiment, an Englishman, was wounded in an attack and was lying on the ground amongst dead and wounded men. At dusk the gunners put down a barrage on the Jap positions so that the wounded could be brought in. Unfortunately the Company Commander had died from his wounds.

A few parties of Japs eventually succeeded in infiltrating onto the plain near Palel where there was an air strip, and Hurribombers were called up to help the Gurkhas and Borders withstand their fanatical attacks. But as General Slim says in his book, 'The 20th Division had successfully withstood heavy assaults and continuous pressure for over two months and to ease the strain on it, the Corps Commander relieved it on the Palel front by the 23rd Division.' So we dropped down from the ridge on to an area of the Plain near Imphal for a short break and experienced a touch of civilisation. There was a YMCA canteen nearby run by two British ladies who provided tea, cakes and chat. Dick's memory is better than mine; he says that they had just four gramophone records to amuse us. 'Apple Blossom Time' by the Andrews Sisters and a Bing Crosby number were two of them. It was a welcome break but it lasted for no more than about ten days as we were soon called on to support infantry whose task was to cut off the Japs as they retreated in disarray after their unsuccessful attempt to capture Kohima.

Kohima at that time was a small town in the Naga Hills lying astride the only line of communication between Dimapur and Imphal. Within days of the 'March on Delhi' this road had been

There seems nothing wrong with the morale of this group of F Troop gunners and signallers as they rested on the plain

cut in several places as a result of the Japanese lightning sweep through the jungle which laid siege to Imphal and the surrounding plain. Since then all our supplies had been dropped from the air. Much has been written about the battle for Kohima and why the Japanese didn't by-pass it and concentrate their efforts on the main base of Dimapur. I had passed through Kohima on my way up to the front and can only say I was glad not to have been involved in the battle to take it. However, the failure of the Japanese to capture the town is worth a mention here, as some of us were sent to help in blocking their retreat from the town. Lt. General Sato, who commanded the 31st Division which was broken at Kohima, was sacked by the High Command for his failure, as well as for his insubordination. A Japanese commentator later described the battles for Kohima and Imphal as the worst defeat ever chronicled in the annals of war. It may not generally be known that the very moving epitaph which has been used for many years at remembrance services was first inscribed on the memorial stone at Kohima.

> When you go home,
> Tell them of us and say,
> For your tomorrow,
> We gave our today.

The war cemetery and new Cathedral have been given prominent places in the rebuilt town.

The demand for OP signallers had been heavy during May and Infantry conditions were not as conducive to letter writing as duty at the gun position. I find that I began a letter on 19 June: 'Well, I have arrears of letters to answer, seeing that this week I haven't had much opportunity.' I also spent half of the letter saying how much I was interested in a Government plan to train 70,000 new teachers to be recruited from servicemen after the war, which I expect I had seen in the *SEAC* newspaper. It was good that we were in this way stimulated to turn our thoughts to the peace. I concluded: 'The second front is going well for which we have to thank God. The Yanks are doing marvellously too in the Pacific. We are smartening them up around here as well. They suffer a lot

They shall not pass

The memorial at Kohima

more casualties than us. Land, sea or air are all the same. See you have a good time at Blackpool.' (My parents' annual holiday was usually spent there.)

I notice that I didn't mention the monsoon which must have been causing us extra problems by that time and the perpetual dampness may have been a factor in the trouble I encountered. My memory doesn't help me very much, so I have to rely on my mucker Sid Burden. Sid says that I was with him and Jimmy Hussey at an OP with the Gurkhas in the Ukhrul area. Captain Barney, our Troop Commander, was with us. The monsoon rain had us slipping and sliding through a patch of elephant grass when I collapsed with an attack of malaria. 'You were pretty groggy,' Sid tells me, 'but we managed to get to our position for the night and Jimmy and me made you comfortable with a makeshift shelter of leaves.' Major Morrell, our Battery Commander, arrived the next day in his jeep and took me off with him, I assume to the Imphal airstrip where I was evacuated to the Base Hospital at Comilla, to be treated by Queen Alexandra's Nurses.

General Slim in his book says that air evacuation did more in the 14th Army to save lives than any other agency. Light aircraft picked up casualties on air strips cut out of the jungle or paddy field within a mile or two of the fighting and flew them to the supply strip many miles further back. Here the casualties were transferred to Dakotas returning empty from the supply run and flown direct to a general hospital. One such hospital took in during 1944 and 1945 over eleven thousand British casualties, often in their filthy bloodstained battledress, straight from the front line. I am amazed to read that the total deaths in that hospital were only twenty-three.

Since the introduction of daily tablets of mepacrine and disciplinary measures like wearing our shirts and long trousers before sunset, the incidence of malaria had declined considerably. Sleeping under mosquito nets would have been beneficial but this was hardly ever possible for the forward troops. However, the mosquito net is no respecter of persons as Bill Slim was also in hospital about the same time, as he says, 'by an attack of malaria with some unpleasant complications.' He honestly admits that he had not practised what he preached, and had washed in the open after sunset, thus disobeying his own orders.

Whilst I was in hospital my comrades on 20 Division were completing the mopping up of stragglers from the Jap 15th and 31st Divisions. Apparently their High Command had hoped they would make a stand at Ukhrul, but they were so weak and exhausted, this didn't happen. One memory is clear from just before my bout of malaria, when emaciated, skeleton-like Japs retreating from Kohima were being picked up by our Infantry. I saw one who had been shot through the foot and who was helped along by, I think, one of the Devons, who had given him a cigarette. This treatment is in contrast to the stories we heard about the cruel and inhumane actions of the Japs towards our prisoners.

I believe it took about three weeks to get fit again at Comilla and then it was back to the Imphal Plain. The monsoon rains had hampered operations and it was much quieter now with the Japs having trekked back to Burma from whence they had come in March. We were soon to follow them, but first came an unexpected leave in the big city – Calcutta.

The monsoon brings the war to a halt for a while for F troop gunners

CHAPTER II

Leave in Calcutta
and the SA again

I HAVE ALREADY REFERRED to the hazardous road from Imphal back to the railhead at Dimapur, but I didn't have to worry about it as a Dakota was found with some space to take a number of us to Dum Dum airfield near Calcutta. It was almost like what is now known as 'a package deal' as accommodation for two weeks was also laid on for us at an Army camp in the outskirts of the city. I wasn't going to refuse this chance to experience the real India for the first time. The city was large even then, but it has grown considerably since partition in 1947, when millions of Hindus flooded into the city from neighbouring areas which were to become part of Muslim Pakistan. In recent years Calcutta has become known world-wide for the relief and medical work of Mother Teresa and her Sisters of Mercy.

A letter I wrote to my parents when I arrived tells its own story.

20th October, 1944

Well, I guess you'll be pleased that at last I find myself on leave in Calcutta just a week after arriving back at the Troop from Hospital. I was lucky enough to be able to fly here in just under two hours instead of the wearisome road and rail journey of a few days length. I managed to find a bed vacant at the Salvation Army Hostel here. I was supposed to go to a billet arranged by the Army, but just like Army organisation the place was full up, so that gave me the opportunity to find the Hostel and a vacancy, for which I was glad. I'm in a room with three beds and one of the other lads is a Salvationist. He comes from Belfast Citadel Corps and spoke well of John Rout-ledge when he was CO there. His name is McGuiness. It's probably just as well my leave was delayed as it's getting cooler here now although it's enough to make you sweat a bit. If I'd come here say in June it would have been unbearable. The main streets of Calcutta are like an English city, except that there are loads of Indians shouting, 'Shine, sahib,' or 'Books, papers, sahib,' or again, 'baksheesh, sahib.' I hope on Sunday, or perhaps before then, for the first time since Durban, to attend an SA meeting and probably make an attempt at playing a cornet.

So cheerio and God Bless for now.

Getting a place in the SA Hostel was a real God-send for me, although even if I'd stayed at the Army camp I would have sought out the SA hall and fellow Salvationists. I realise that this would be a strange priority for most young men in this situation, being let loose for the first time in an Asian city. But for Christians, the Church (that is the people, not the building) is the body of Christ and it is appropriate that they should be drawn together in this way. That is not to take a 'holier than thou' attitude, but isn't it true in general that people of like minds are attracted together, and to some extent everyone has his or her 'centre of worship'. So during this fortnight I found myself quite frequently at the SA along with about thirty-five other servicemen from all three services, some of whom were stationed nearby and others who like me were on leave.

Of course, I didn't neglect to get around to see what the city offered the 'tourist'. I enjoyed the hustle and bustle of the main shopping street, Chowringhee, and the particular fascination of Firpo's where it seemed the whole of the East was represented in its snack bars and restaurant. Then in the October sunshine I savoured the relative peace of the Maidan, strolling past the Victoria Memorial, St Peter's Church and of course Fort William, built by the East India Company and interesting because of the folklore surrounding the 'Black Hole' incident in 1756. I suppose 'The Black Hole of Calcutta' is a little bit of the history of the Empire which most children remember from school, at any rate in my day. It seems that the name was coined after a large number of the English got themselves imprisoned in a very small, airless and damp kind of dungeon, following a successful attack on the Fort by a young Nawab of the time. Only a handful survived the ordeal. The famous Hoogly river which runs nearby was muddy brown then, as it is now. The large and impressive Indian Museum is just off Chowringhee, but I couldn't tell you a thing about it now, and to be honest I may not have been too interested then. It's a pity that most of us had the attitude that, having been brought 6,000 miles to do a job, all we wanted was to get on with it and return home as soon as possible. This meant that after the initial excitement had worn off, we didn't take the interest in our surroundings that a modern-day tourist or back-packer would take. A pity really, as I would love now to retrace my steps through the continent, but it would take more stamina than I seem to possess. A few veterans have managed it on well planned excursions run mainly by the British Legion. Good luck to them, I say.

I have said already that the Salvation Army had been planted in many countries of the Empire during the latter part of the last century. Calcutta had therefore been a prominent centre of activity for about sixty years before I arrived. I found that the style of worship, music and message at the Central Corps was similar to that in other Corps where my travels had taken me – Preston, Salisbury, Woolwich and Durban. In other words, it was home from home. Near the end of my leave I wrote home:

30th October 1944

Well, I'm trying to give you a bit extra whilst I'm on leave and have the chance. On 3rd November I'll be making my way back to the Troop, probably by the longest route this time. I really have been uplifted to get to the SA for two week-ends as well as two or three nights in the week, and it will be a great miss for some time to come. I have a little bit of hope that they will manage to get me off for a three week tour of the forward areas. The GOC has sponsored it after he heard the Band play at the presentation of some new instruments. It's something new for an SA Band, all servicemen of course, but if the military want it the chaps will be released. Here's hoping.

This morning I had a good time at the open-air swimming baths which are free to servicemen. It's a grand place; tea, cakes, drinks all on the spot. There's a good film here this week, *Madame Curie*, who discovered radium, and which portrays the tremendous devotion in never giving in when things wouldn't come right. The newsreels of the liberation of Paris and Marseilles too were marvellous.

I hope the letter enclosing the photographs has reached you by now. I expect it will take longer than these air-letter cards.

Well, I hope everything is OK at home. I'll be glad to get hold of that bunch of letters when I arrive back, as well as parcels which I hope are waiting for me. The spell in hospital and now this leave means that I'll feel like a

A studious one taken in Calcutta. Perhaps my thoughts have turned to going back to Burma

'rookie' to F Troop. I'll have to settle down until the next time – leave or whatever it may be. So for the time being, cheerio and God Bless.

I'm afraid I didn't manage to join the Band on their tour. However, my name was put on the Band's mailing list and some time after, when I was over the Burma border, I received a lengthy report of their tour headed 'Dispatches from the Arakan Front'. They had a difficult, tiring but worth-while time visiting Army camps, RAF stations and often small forward units. Most servicemen knew of the 'Sally Ann' and had great respect for it. Many had been thankful for the Red Shield Canteens which were around even in India. So the Band had been welcomed by crowds of supporters as they played and sang the music which conveyed their experience as Christians. There had been many requests for favourite hymns and I'm sure there would be many damp eyes as the familiar words and tunes reminded them of home. The touring Band was made up of twenty-eight servicemen who hailed from Corps as far apart as Edinburgh and Eastbourne. Here is an extract from the diary of the tour:

> For the past five hours we have been steaming down a broad river in a paddle boat. We haven't seen much of the scenery as we have been playing to the British, Indian and Allied servicemen crowded into every available deck space. On the invitation for favourites from our song book we simply haven't been able to keep pace with the many requests from these men on their way back into Burma. How they sang – especially that hymn of childhood memories – 'There is a green hill far away'.
>
> What are these men thinking about? Of the past; what crowded memories must be there. Or of the immediate future with its inherent dangers?

I'm sorry I missed the experience. I have kept a copy of the Band's Newsletter dated April 1945, and it says that well over 350 servicemen and servicewomen spent some time with the Band at the Calcutta Central Corps during those awful years. The same newsletter records the death of one of them, a sailor from the Castleford Corps, and I will conclude this chapter with the following extract from the homily written by the SA Officer who knew him. It puts everything into perspective.

> It is with feelings of real loss that we have heard of the passing of Cliff who was seriously injured in the Ramree Island invasion. Cliff Thompson will be remembered by a great number of his comrades as an earnest sincere Christian gentleman. No man could leave such lasting influences which challenge and inspire us, without a very real experience of the constant companionship of the Christ.
>
> The price of our freedom becomes very heavy when such men as Cliff must give up life itself to win it for us.

CHAPTER 12

Back to Burma
for the chase to Rangoon

M Y NEXT LETTER HOME was dated 12 November 1944, so I reckon I must have got a lift in the fuselage of another Dakota, as if I had gone by road I would not have made it in the time. The letter included the following passage:

> I am allowed to tell you that we are at present resting on the Imphal Plain. So that explains the reason for a recreation room and a few other amenities. We see a concert or a picture now and again. The Band of the North Staffs was giving a programme a few nights ago too and I enjoyed it very much. There's not even the trouble of a black-out so it's not so bad. It doesn't say much for the Japanese Air Force I guess. The Calcutta SA are keeping in touch with me by a monthly newsletter which is good. Pleased you sent the Journal with George Boak's photo. Yes that's the lad who was all through the Creighton School with me. As regards a Commission, I put my name down and had a preliminary test a week ago but I've heard no more about it yet. If I did succeed I suppose it would be the Indian Army I'd be put in, which means no repatriation for three and a half years. Most of the Divisions like mine are Indian. Of course that doesn't mean all the units are made up of Indians, probably about half the troops are British.

By this time the line of communications road from Dimapur to Imphal had been opened with the help of the 5th Indian Division which had been flown in from the Arakan; the Kohima garrison had been relieved by the British 2nd Division and although the Japanese Divisions had been reinforced in the hope of making a stand at Ukhrul, they were being chased back to the Chindwin.

Pursuing them in the monsoon conditions was proving very difficult, as is clear from a quotation from a Brigade War Diary given by the General in his book:

> Hill tracks in a terrible state, either so slippery that men can hardly walk or knee-deep in mud. Administrative difficulties considerable. Half a company took ten hours to carry two stretcher cases four miles. A party of men without packs took seven hours to cover five miles.

The general also records how keen he was to rest as many as possible of the troops who had been engaged since March in coping with the Japanese advance. My leave had been part of this 'treat-

The 'rest camp' at Wangjing. The monsoon trenches are now drying up

ment' as was the rest camp at a place called Wangjing on the edge of the Plain. I have a photo of our camp which shows how we enjoyed the luxury not quite of tents, but of a tarpaulin covered structure, surrounded of course with monsoon trenches which we had to dig ourselves. At least we were able to construct our make-shift beds once more and guard duties were less frequent. The food was better too; I believe we had some bread! An examination of the men who had been in action over the last year had revealed evidence of malnutrition and the powers that be tried to do some-thing about this problem by adding some fresh meat and vegetables to the ration, at any rate while there was some lull in the fighting.

We appreciated our stay at Wangjing mainly for the simple pleasures of food and sleep, but also for the opportunity to see more of each other in the Troop, both gunners and signallers, as in action the signallers were spread about at OPs or out with line parties. The cards came out and some of the more dedicated 'card sharpers' managed to swell their nest-egg for the day of their release by the addition of a few thousand rupees. There must have been a policy to keep boredom at bay from Monday to Friday, as this extract from the letter of 25 November shows:

> It's Saturday afternoon when I'm writing this and I hope to have a restful week-end with no parades except Church parade and of course an anti-mosquito parade when the yellow tablets are given out and they see you get them down. This has been quite a busy week going out on Schemes etc., and getting back when it's almost dark. There is a concert tonight given by a party from another Battery, which will pass a couple of hours away quite well.

By early December we were 'on the road again'. In the Kohima and Imphal battles the Japanese Army had suffered the greatest defeat in its history. Five Divisions had been decimated and many administrative units badly disrupted. The Japanese themselves con-firmed that ninety thousand men had been killed or seriously injured. Only six hundred had been captured, very different from the Eu-ropean War and indicative of the fanatical nature of their soldiers and the propaganda with which they were fed. Our own losses were less than half those of the Japanese, but by the nature of the fighting our heaviest losses were among the Officers and NCOs. Only a few of our men had been captured; those men who were wounded were invariably murdered or left to die. None of our guns was taken, which confirms the policy which was stressed to us that the protection of our perimeters was of paramount importance.

So it was with some confidence that the guns were limbered up and the signalling trucks loaded, ready for the long haul up the well remembered Shenam Pass and down the other side past the familiar names of Moreh and Tamu. The signs of battle were all around us. Nippon Hill, Gibraltar, Scraggy and Malta were all now shorn of trees and looking like the surface of the moon. Why should hundreds of my fellow Cumbrians and Scots from the Border country, as well as Nepalese and Sikhs, be killed or maimed for the sake of territory on a hilltop in this remote part of the world? If I have an answer it is a simple one, that it is something to do with man's sin, selfishness, pride and lust for power, particularly in high places. In this century the ordinary people of many nations have suffered at the hands of their leaders. At Tamu and in the Kabaw Valley as we passed through on our way to the Chindwin, there were grisly signs of dozens of Japanese killed or starved to death and half buried in the clearings and even in the village streets. I must admit that at that time I never thought that mothers or wives back in Tokyo, Kobe or Nagasaki were receiving telegrams bringing the same sad news that was being brought to parents and loved ones of those in the Border country. We were aware that the Japanese, led by War-lords, had been trained from school for aggressive action and that it had been instilled into them that dying for the Emperor was a very noble deed. Because our western democratic and Christian culture was so different, we really felt there was something inhuman about them. I'm afraid we had little sorrow for them as we saw their lifeless bodies lying in the dust. I can only be glad that the philosophy, culture and direction of the Japanese nation seems to have changed for the good in the last fifty years and that their leaders have even apologised for atrocities committed in the first half of the century as a result of their expansionist war aims.

The General had given orders to his Corps Commander to pursue the enemy on each of the routes Imphal – Tiddim – Kalemyo – Kalewa and, if opportunity arose, to seize Kalewa and establish a bridgehead across the Chindwin river. Our next stop therefore was Kalemyo where we prepared for the advance into the Burmese Plain across the major rivers running north and south from their source in the Himalayas. But first the only Christmas dinner out East which sticks in my memory. We erected a large tarpaulin for a tent and actually sat at tables to be served good Christmas fare by the Sergeants and Officers. A modicum of alcohol was available and I remember that cigars were handed round. As we were not used to food and drink in such quantity and richness, I'm afraid that a number of us paid the price for it a few hours later. A great cheer went up as a spotter plane flew by with a banner attached to its tail saying, 'Happy Christmas to all'. This was a welcome gesture from an Air Observation Post Squadron who had mustered at Salisbury after my own 651 Squadron had left for Algeria.

While we had been resting, the enemy had been pushed back to the Chindwin and bridgeheads had been established on the eastern bank. We had to thank a considerable number of troops from the Empire (now the Commonwealth) for this success. The 11th East African Division and the 5th Indian Division were the spearhead. They were men from the African colonies as well as from various parts of India, Punjabis and Dogras. These troops along with the Royal Air Force, who patrolled incessantly, enabled our engineers to erect a floating Bailey bridge over the Chindwin. Indian sappers and miners assembled the spans under cover in the Myittha River, floated them to the Chindwin, and put the bridge in position in twenty-eight hours. Its length was 1,154 feet, then the longest Bailey bridge in the world. The bridge was attacked from the air and two Japanese bombers were brought down.

So, early in January 1945, we gathered ourselves together, crossed the bridge without mishap (strange to see some barrage balloons in position) and prepared for the more difficult crossing of the Irrawaddy and the pursuit of the Japs through central Burma to Rangoon, a mere 600 miles.

CHAPTER 13

Approach to the Irrawaddy

ADAPTABILITY, flexibility and movement were now required of us as we were confronted by very different conditions on our way towards the Irrawaddy and Central Burma. From the Kabaw Valley and the Chin Hills which had been our defensive line, we now emerged into flat scrub and dry river tributaries which we knew as *chaungs*. These *chaungs* were sometimes wide enough for us to use as ready made gun emplacements and our gunners liked them, not only for the protection they gave from enemy shells, but because less digging was required. The sandy bottom of the *chaung* also made it easy to dig if this was necessary. But unlike our previous experience, to stay in one place for a week or ten days was now a long time. Our warfare became very mobile and a little more 'European' in style. Tanks came into their own in the new situation, and as the Infantry pressed forward, so we were right behind them with close support.

We were now well over three hundred miles from the main railhead at Dimapur and it was planned that we would be supplied largely by air. The Corps Headquarters staffs had a massive task of organisation to achieve a good result, and I have read since that the General was none too pleased when his superiors pinched three Squadrons of Dakotas to help the Chinese in their fight against the same enemy. However, apart from the supplies, it was good for our morale every few days to see scores of parachutes floating down to provide our life-line. It was an eerie feeling in the peace and quiet of 'stand-to', each man wrapped up in his own thoughts, to see, in the red of the setting sun, the discarded white parachutes gently waving in the warm breeze and hanging like shrouds from a dozen trees. Then with 'stand down' called we would solemnly stroll back to our bed spaces to reminisce for a while, before finding a few hours of oblivion until the whisper in our ear, 'Stand-to, mate' as dawn began to streak across the sky to start another day.

It was the middle of January. The monsoon had been over for about three months; the lesser rivers were dry or down to a trickle, the sun was relentless and hot. Every wheel of gun-carriage or truck threw up clouds of dust from the non-metalled roads and with our bush hats firmly planted on our heads and a handkerchief tied round our nose and mouth, we could have been mistaken for extras in a John Wayne film. I think I can say that we loved our bush hats and only wore our 'tin hats' when absolutely necessary. We felt distinctive and special in them and were able to express our own individuality in the way we pulled the felt about to make the shape that seemed to suit each personality.

The main task for 20 Division after crossing the Bailey bridge on the Chindwin was to capture Monywa, a fairly large town by Burmese standards. From Monywa the Division would be well placed to seek a crossing of the Irrawaddy which turned westwards from Mandalay to join up with the River Chindwin, some miles to the south of the town.

First on our route was the town of Budalin which gave us an impression of Burma in all its mysticism. It was a quite beautiful town full of pagodas and surrounded by flat open country, but at this time was unfortunately occupied by a garrison of about a hundred Japanese. The Northants in 32 Brigade, whom we were supporting at this time, soon boxed them into a small perimeter, and forty of them made their escape during the night, which led to some interesting correspondence after the war between the two commanders. Louis Allen in his book *Burma – the longest war*, tells of how the Japanese commander after the war wrote to the Northants Commanding Officer to say that he felt that he must have intentionally overlooked their retreat and greatly appreciated that the lives of men, many of whom were wounded, had been spared. The British Commander replied, 'I feel sure the reason you were not fired on was that by the light of flares it is not easy to distinguish friend from foe and, knowing there were Gurkhas

behind you, our fire was withheld rather than risk casualties to our own troops.'

The next day, about 10 January 1945, as our guns and trucks processed along the main street of this first Burmese town which we had helped to liberate, we were thrilled with the cheering and waving of so many happy people. No. I'm joking!! In fact we soon realised that we would have to settle for almost complete indifference from the Burmese in most of the towns and villages that we captured.

It was about this time that we were favoured with an open-air cinema show and had a chance to see newsreels of the liberation of Paris and Brussels, when the troops were mobbed by the populace, with flowers and an abundance of kisses. 'Blessed is he that expecteth nothing, for he will not be disappointed' (Alexander Pope, I believe) could be said to have been our philosophy after our experience in Budalin. Anyway, I'm sure we enjoyed our film show, the first since Imphal, and Don actually remembers that one of the films was a British propaganda effort to show how everybody at home was doing their bit for the troops at the front. It was called *Rosie the Rivetter* and is memorable for the bouncing-ball technique to help us to sing the words of the song with the same title.

It was at Budalin and Monywa that I first sensed the influence of Buddhism on this race of people, living as they did sandwiched between India to the west and China to the east but with topographical barriers from both their neighbours, and existing for centuries as a very distinct people. On a quiet evening there was something magical about the atmosphere as the temple bells tinkled, the setting sun reflecting from the golden and jewelled pagodas. Hearing the measured tread of a line of saffron robed monks making their way past the *chinthes* standing erect and forbidding at the entrance to each pagoda, there to approach with obeisance the statue of the impressive looking golden Buddha confronting them. Then, as the sun set, the brilliant Burma moon in a clear star lit sky rose in the east to maintain the magical glow well into the night. One of our company was able to give me a photographic record of this introduction to the real Burma.

The reality of what we were about was very different as the next few weeks would reveal. The Division's next objective was the important town of Monywa, a centre of communications by rail and river. I have no memory of it, but it is etched on the mind of Dick Williams who went with an OP party to join the Northants attacking the town. He says they were shelled constantly and had to suffer Jap 'jitter parties' outside the perimeter as a prelude to outright attacks with bayonets drawn and yelling, '*Banzai*'. He later walked through the town, which had been devastated.

After Monywa the 4th/10th Gurkhas had a considerable success in clearing the town of Myinmu on the bank of the Irrawaddy in preparation for the Divisional crossing. The 2nd Borders then took over the town and orders were given to probe the shores of the river for likely crossing places. Their experiences first in ridding the north and west shore of Japanese and then seeking a site for a bridgehead across the river, almost a mile wide in some parts, is so well written up in *The Little Men* by K. W. Cooper, that I can only recommend it to those readers who would wish to know of the horrors of fighting such an enemy at close quarters. The chapter 'Satpangon – Profile of a Battle' is a vivid description of how they had to winkle out the enemy from defensive bunkers which they had built in the centre of the village. The utter determination of the Japs to hold on to the western shore of the river and to kill or be killed made the job of the Borders very difficult and they lost many officers and men in the process. It is some satisfaction that shells from our guns were of some help to them. The skills of the Japs in 'going to ground' so that after the artillery barrage they

Don Turner April 1945 in Calcutta: En route from Burma to Korseong

could come out fighting, is an illustration of what the Infantry had to face all over Burma. I repeat my admiration for the courage and selflessness of these men.

However, Satpangon was eventually cleared of Japs in hand to hand fighting and the Division could made plans for the crossing of the river.

CHAPTER 14

Now for the crossing

THE OLD SONG, 'On the road to Mandalay', written in 1916 when British troops could expect postings to remote parts of the Empire including Burma, is a favourite at the Burma Star Reunions. The chorus goes:

> Come ye back to Mandalay, where the old flotilla lay,
> Can't you hear the paddles chunking from Rangoon to
> Mandalay,
> On the road to Mandalay, where the flying fishes play,
> And the dawn comes up like thunder out of China 'cross
> the bay.

This 'road', the river Irrawaddy, has been to the Burmese over the centuries the main artery on which their life depended, in much the same way as our waterways and canals served us before mechanical transport and the building of the M1. It is interesting that as I write, movements are springing up in the UK protesting at the increasing number of road building projects which churn up the countryside. This song conjures up a romantic picture of a by-gone era which will never return, not only to Britain but to many other 'developing countries'. In 1944 however, the Irrawaddy was still a major life-line as many roads were little more than dirt tracks and the railways although existing were limited in scope. One can understand how some of the great rivers of Asia, the Ganges, Indus, Brahmaputra and Irrawaddy, all with their source in the mighty Himalayas, came to be worshipped. They played such an important part in the lives of the primitive people.

Mandalay was of course a prestige target for the 14th Army, but General Slim was more concerned in inflicting a major defeat on

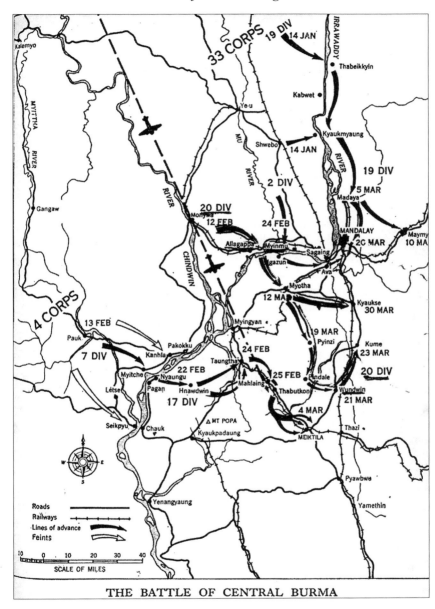

THE BATTLE OF CENTRAL BURMA

Battle of Central Burma

the Japanese forces as he realised that only by doing this could he hope to reach a southern Burma port, preferably Rangoon, before the monsoon broke in May. The line of communication from Dimapur in Assam was so long and the continued air lifting of supplies so problematical, that a port into which supplies could be poured was absolutely essential before the monsoon hindered the Army's progress. The worse scenario might be that the Army would have to limp back to the Chindwin and hold the India/Burma border again. Time was relatively short and it was a long way to Rangoon, over four hundred miles. Slim had hoped to defeat the main body of the enemy on the Shewbo plain to the north and west of Mandalay but from captured documents he realised that this was not going to happen. Unfortunately, Kimura was leaving only a screen of troops to the west of the Irrawaddy and was banking all on throwing us back into the river when we tried to establish bridgeheads. The Japanese 15th Army had been receiving fresh reinforcements since the Imphal encounter when they had lost over 65,000 men and Kimura issued a rallying call for what he called 'The Battle of the Irrawaddy Shore'.

Maintaining his objective to inflict a major defeat on the Japanese, Slim now realised that he would first have to cross the Irrawaddy in some force. He says in his book, 'I do not think any modern army has ever attempted the opposed crossing of a great river with so little. We had few power craft and were especially weak on outboard engines. The only equipment my army had in full supply was, as ever, brains, hardihood and courage.' Yet the General at times had his doubts.

> In no other theatre would an army have been launched on such a task with such pitiful equipment. Success depended on what? Luck? Imagination is a necessity for a General, but it must be controlled imagination. At times I regained control of mine by an effort of will, of concentration on the immediate job in hand. And then I walked once more among my soldiers, and I, who should have inspired them, not for the first or last time drew courage from them. Men like these could not fall. God helps those who help themselves. He would help us.

His Chief Engineer had worked wonders by establishing a boat building yard on the Chindwin using the teak trees which were in abundance and the expertise of 'Elephant Bill' with his magnificent beasts of burden. Hundreds of wooden boats and rafts came out of this yard in double quick time and these and rubber dinghies fitted with outboard motors would have to take most of the men and their supplies across the fast flowing river nearly a mile wide in places. Powered craft such as those used in the Rhine crossing were in short supply. The picture of a specially converted Bren-gun carrier using oil drums as floats indicates how ingenuity and the philosophy of making the best of what was available prevailed. With the capture of Monywa by the 20 Division, the Irrawaddy came into view and the need for some of us to be over there with the Borders and Gurkhas as they strove to hold on to a few miles of the western shore was very likely. The Japs would soon have their own guns in place and they would need to be countered. Who would be in the first wave? We were soon to discover.

As it happened two of my close muckers and myself were heavily involved in the establishing of the bridgehead. Dick Williams had joined F Troop at Witok, and he and I soon found that we had much in common, more in common than the things which divided us. In civvy-street we were separated by as many miles as it was possible to be in England. Dick came from a little village called Nancledra near Penzance, probably about five hundred miles from the Scottish border where Carlisle is situated. I had been used to sitting on my backside as a wages clerk, but Dick, all six foot two of him, had dreams of patrolling the Cornish lanes as a policeman, although with his call up pending he had taken a job as an assistant in a shoe shop. I could be right in describing him as a soft spoken gentle giant, whereas I was only a few inches over five foot, but nevertheless could occasionally be a bit awkward with authority, particularly of the 'spit and polish' kind. In talking about our parents, we found that we were both only children from rather sheltered and clearly Christian backgrounds. Methodism was very strong in Cornwall and Dick's father was an elder in the local Chapel. Dick himself had been recruited as Secretary for the Sunday

School at the Chapel. So our early years had inculcated in us similar standards and outlook on life. My other close mucker, Don Turner, had been one of the reinforcements to the Troop as we rested at Wangjing. Don was 'about my size' and from South London. He had had an association with a Church Covenanter group and since leaving school had been interested in the electrical and mechanical field. Whilst at Wangjing he volunteered for Driver Operator VCP and luckily for him, when he reported for duty at the Battery Office, was told that he was not required after all. He was perhaps a bit naive as usually the watchword was 'don't volunteer for anything'. He discovered after the war that there was a sting in the tail and that he had volunteered for signalling at a Visual Control Point which specialised in targeting enemy positions. It could have been more hazardous than the task of a troop signaller and with hindsight he was glad nothing came of it.

Slim had to keep his opposite number guessing and he produced a bold, and he hoped secret, plan to destroy the main body of troops around Mandalay and stop them from being reinforced, by striking for their main supply base at Melktila forty miles to the south. He decided to send 4 Corps through the thickly wooded Gangaw valley to appear suddenly on the Irrawaddy bank near Pakokku, and race to take the airfield at Melktila and then the town itself. His gamble depended on complete surprise, so he took various steps to conceal his intentions including a phoney Corps HQ at Tamu supplying false intelligence to the enemy listening posts. His plan was brilliantly executed and fully successful to the extent that when the 19th and 20th Divisions were surrounding Mandalay, 4 Corps were already besieging Melktila, over-running the supply dumps and restricting the escape route for the troops to the north.

As I said earlier, the Japanese commander was hoping to guess where we would cross the river and throw us back into the water when we had crossed. I'm sure I wasn't aware of it at the time but the General has since revealed that because of the lack of supplies and equipment it was only possible for one Division in each Corps to cross at a time, which to say the least must have severely handicapped him in his planning. Slim's plan was to get Kimura to think

A scruffy group wearing cap comforters

that the main crossings would be to the north of Mandalay so that he would be caught off balance when 4 Corps appeared in the south and struck for Melktika. So, early in January, the 19th Division north of Mandalay began probing the Irrawaddy shore for suitable crossing places and on the 14th, an Infantry Company crossed at a point about fifty miles from Mandalay. Over the next few days, crossings were made at points nearer Mandalay and most of the Division was over within a week. The Japanese reacted by calling up troops from two Divisions with additional artillery and, for three weeks to early February, hit hard at the bridgeheads, but to no avail. Slim praises the part the RAF played at this time in silencing the enemy artillery, many pilots flying five or six sorties a day.

As soon as it was clear that the 19th Division had held on to their bridgehead, it was the turn of 20 Division to cross to the south of Mandalay and so put the town in pincer-like grasp. A crossing point for our Brigade was chosen near a village called Myinmu, about twenty miles from Mandalay. The date was 12 February 1945, and from then until the end of the month was probably the most memorable period of my time out east.

CHAPTER 15

On the road to Mandalay

O N THE NIGHT of 12 February 1945, Bombardier Stafford in charge of F Troop signals, along with a small group of signallers including Dick Williams, prepared for the crossing of the Irrawaddy. Wireless communications between Observation Posts with the Infantry and the Command Post at the gun position had never been easy in the jungle conditions in the hills on the India/Burma border, but it began to be more reliable as we advanced over the plains of central Burma. Nevertheless we always preferred to lay a cable and use a telephone link where this was possible and it was decided that Bom Stafford and a small group should attempt to lay a line on the bed of the river. For most of the day the lucky few could be seen cleaning rifles and sten guns, loading their small packs with rations and other necessities, making sure those with wireless sets had fully charged batteries and, last but not least, arranging a workable system of cable reels to splay out the line on to the river bed. Then at dusk, their bush hats discarded for the more convenient cap comforters and looking, and no doubt feeling, more like Commandos, they disappeared into the back of a truck for a short ride to the mighty river. Dick remembers that he went over with another signaller and two gunners in a boat rowed by a Burmese man. They drifted a bit with the current but landed unopposed on the other side. The only source of communication for a few days was the wireless set until the land line party linked up with them. After they had gone, the rest of us got down to our tasks in the Command Post preparing for a night to be spent lobbing shells over the river to keep the heads of the Japs down, while our mates clambered up the sandy bank of the river to hold on to some precious bit of land in the face of the enemy.

About a week later orders were on the board for the signalling party to relieve Dick and his band over the river, and Don and yours truly were included. We were to take a 19 wireless set, the smallest one going at the time, which when on the move could be carried on the back of one of us, whilst the other would plug in the headset and make contact with the command post. I don't know which was the worst role but in any case we changed over occasionally. Like the first party we set off at midnight for the west bank of the river. The bridgehead on the other side was holding by now and the organisation for finding our boats and embarking seemed to be 'well oiled'. We flopped into one of the rubber dinghies fitted with an outboard motor and set off for the far shore at an angle across the river because of the strong current. We were heading for a distant dim red light and our fingers were crossed as we had already heard of a similar party whose motors had packed up in mid stream and who had had to paddle like mad to reach the other side. Unfortunately they landed on the beach several hundred yards from the guiding light and had to cope with a Jap patrol in the area. However, our outboard motors purred away and we soon found ourselves wading through the shallows to be allocated a spot well up the beach where we could dig in and try to get some sleep before first light. Don and I were propped up at either end of the trench we had dug, the 19 set between our legs, and shivering either because of the cold night or from the fear that the proximity of shells and the sounds of battle brought about.

Dawn came, it seemed rather tardily, and we found that we were to join the Northants at a position up the beach about a mile away. Trudging up the beach, we caught a glimpse of a couple of our Troop wearily and it seemed a bit shell shocked, heading for the dinghies to be shipped back to the gun position and a few days' rest. Our OP position with the Northants was in a spot we called 'the pimple' where a dry *chaung* met the Irrawaddy. We had to scramble over some half buried Jap bodies to be given a slit trench in the sandy ground at the top. We arrived to the sound of the Northants mortar company giving covering fire to their rifle company who were poised ready to attack a group of the enemy who had infiltrated the position. We found that for the next week we had to live with the sickly smell of rotting corpses in our nostrils. We spent a good deal of our time on 'the pimple' keeping our heads down as the Jap gunners with their 'whizz bangs' had a go at the defenders of this vital position on the bridgehead. We could hear the shells being released from their 105 mm guns but not a sound followed until the last seconds when the shell exploded, hopefully not too near us.

One particular incident is imprinted in the memory of Don and myself. The Battery Commander had detailed his Adjutant, a Captain Figgis, to accompany us on our expedition to the bridgehead. This was most unusual as we usually had with us the Troop Commander, Captain Barney, or one of the other Officers whom we knew quite well. We didn't know Captain Figgis from Adam as he was usually a logistics man and rarely out of the Battery Command Post. However, we had Captain Figgis, an unknown quantity, to cope with and soon after our arrival at the pimple we were called out to accompany a platoon of the Northants who were detailed to investigate and eliminate a supposed Jap bunker a few hundred yards outside the perimeter. We left the crater-strewn area around our slit trenches, set off in the direction of the bunker and found cover amidst a considerable patch of elephant grass where the Northants paused to assess the position. I had the wireless set slung on my back and Don trotted along behind keeping in touch with the command post at the battery through the headphones. Apparently there was little to see of any enemy activity in the direction of the bunker but it was decided to put a few of our shells into it. After asking for a ranging shot or two with smoke, Captain Figgis wanted a good look to see if the guns were on target. His physique was lean, gaunt and tall, about a foot higher than the elephant grass and Don and I, operating the set in the cover of the grass, looked at each other askance as the bold Captain stood to his full height and surveyed the scene through his binoculars. We expected him to cop a sniper's bullet at any moment. However the bunker was plastered with 25-pounder shells and if it was occupied we certainly didn't see any survivors. As well as this kind of support for the

Infantry, Captain Figgis kept us busy with trips to the edge of the perimeter to enable our guns to range for what were called SOS tasks, so that in the event of a surprise attack on any part of our defences, the command post had everything worked out in advance and could speedily lay down a barrage. On one of these trips Don remembers a fanatical attack on the infantry trenches, the Japs as usual blowing bugles and shouting their war cry: *'Banzai, Banzai.'* The Japs had few tanks but they had assembled all the artillery they could muster in support of their attacks on the bridgehead, but the 'poor bloody infantry' held firm and gradually increased their foothold on the eastern shore.

Thankfully, after about a week on the pimple we were relieved by signallers from E Troop and returned to the main bridgehead ready to find a dinghy to take us back to the gun position. Don reminds me of an incident while we waited there in the comparative safety of the bridgehead Commander's enclosure. The E Troop forward observation officer, Captain Little, out with a patrol of the Northants, had run into an ambush and was desperately trying to get through to the gun position to call down some supporting fire. The gun position radio operator was having difficulty with the weak signal and kept repeating, 'Say again,' to the fire orders from Captain Little. Hearing this on our set, Don interrupted to say, 'Through me,' and relayed the orders via Captain Figgis using the more reliable phone line under the river. The guns were then able to provide smoke cover to enable the patrol to escape the ambush but tragically not before the Northants commander was killed. An E Troop signaller, 'Tubby' Morn, was also caught in the Jap fire as he crossed the *chaung* and subsequently had to have a leg amputated. Captain Little was promoted to Major and awarded the Military Cross. Don's quick reaction to the situation, and the fact that our line under the river worked well, could well have saved others in that patrol from serious injury. It is interesting to record in mentioning this incident that the first F Troop signalling party over the Irrawaddy had experienced trouble with the line they had laid on the bed of the river, and Bom Stafford had swum out to undertake repairs. We were all glad that our likeable, conscientious and indeed modest Bombardier was later awarded the Military Medal for the part he played in the campaign to maintain communications in difficult conditions between the guns and the forward observation posts. General Slim in his book pays tribute to the dedication of the Artillery Officers who were at these posts alongside the Infantry, a high proportion of whom were casualties. If he was here to ask, I'm sure he would include the signallers in his commendation.

Don and I with Captain Figgis (whom we never saw any more) found our allotted dinghy to take us back over the river to join the Troop and 28/76 Battery of which we were a part, who were now preparing to pile into the well established bridgehead. The Japs had gone all out to throw 20 Division back into the water, including some suicidal attacks on our positions. Their brave attempts had cost them nearly a thousand men and in the one week 21 to 27 February our bulldozers had buried five hundred of them in the soft sands of the Irrawaddy shore. The Divisional crossings had drawn troops from the Mandalay defences and had also prevented the enemy from reinforcing the troops coming to the defence of Meiktila to the south. In this area Slim had planned to put 4 Corps across the river shortly after our own crossing. His plan to send this Corps secretly through the heavily wooded Gangaw Valley, which I summarised in the last chapter, worked perfectly and by early March, with the help of airborne landings, 4 Corps were surrounding Meiktila and were on course to capture five small airfields which were going to be vital for supplying the 14th Army for its last phase before the monsoon in May, the drive on Rangoon. So almost simultaneously, 19 Division of 33 Corps in the north were pounding the defences of Mandalay Hill and 20 Division were sweeping round the south of the town to cut the road and rail links with Rangoon, whilst 4 Corps, almost fifty miles further south, were completing the encirclement of the by now bewildered 15th and 33rd Japanese Armies.

CHAPTER 16

Mandalay and the race to Rangoon

BY THE END of March 1945 we found ourselves astride the road and railway from Mandalay to the south, at a place called Kyaukse. The place had recently been looted and Don and I remember we came across a Post Office which was deserted and picked up a few documents which were scattered about the floor. Although the aim of 14th Army was to reach Rangoon before the monsoon in less than two months' time, our Divisional Commander felt that the 9th Field Regiment could have a few days' break, so we welcomed some full nights of sleep and sorted ourselves out after the hectic weeks since Christmas. We even had a birthday to celebrate. Here's an extract from the divisional commander's message.

SPECIAL PLATOON SHEET APRIL 1ST 1945

DIVISIONAL COMMANDER'S MESSAGE TO ALL RANKS
20TH INDIAN DIVISION'S FOURTH BIRTHDAY

With the capture of Kyaukse and the opening of the main road from Mandalay to Meiktilla, our Division and the fine troops attached to it have completed the first stage of the first phase of the battle for the reconquest of Burma.

To all of you, no matter what branch of service you belong to, I send my congratulations and thanks for a truly magnificent achievement, only accomplished so successfully by hard fighting, guts and everyone's determination to succeed.

All our commanders have repeatedly expressed to me their great admiration for the fighting spirit, speed and audacity of the 20th Division's operations. The Army Commander told me that even if we did not capture Mandalay itself, it was largely due to our operations, which he classed as superb, that Mandalay was captured so quickly. We all know that, of course, but it is nice to realise that others appreciate it. I will not eulogise any more but you can all feel that you have the right to be very pleased indeed with yourselves – a very pleasant feeling to have – and that you have enhanced the very high reputation we had already so justly earned in the battle of the Kabaw Valley and Manipur in 1943 and 1944.

Today April 1st, 1945 – I'm afraid this message will not reach you until later – is our fourth birthday as a Division and it has been my great pride and honour not only to have raised the Division, but to have commanded it for these three years. . .

As you know, the Japanese Army in Burma in this last year has suffered nothing but defeat upon defeat. The Fourteenth Army has never stoppped chasing it whatever the weather and then country. The Japs have now two alternatives, to cut their losses and withdraw at once before the monsoon breaks in the middle of May to Siam or Malay, or to go on committing suicide inside Burma. In either case we must go on chasing them. . .

So that is the second phase to which we are re-committed, chasing the Japs out of Burma. It may involve hard fighting; at some places it may be a walk-over, but whatever it is, there is no use in glossing over to you the unpleasant fact that the weather will be foul all the time – hot, sticky, and later wet and that many parts of the country we shall go over will be foul. I've never asked you to make a special effort in vain, and I know that, however beastly the conditions, all ranks will go all out to get cracking after the Japs, after the week's stand-easy of a sort that we are to get till April the 8th.

Let us take as our motto – 'Sword in Hand' – with grins on our faces and smiles in our hearts – to Rangoon.

The very best luck to you all.

Douglas Gracey

By now Mandalay was in the hands of 19 Division so it was decided to give us a 'day trip'. We piled into our 3-tonners, took some items from the American K ration pack such as cheese and biscuits and disgorged from the trucks in a central square of the town. Things seemed to be getting back to normal with a few shops or market stall holders ready to do business with their new clientele, so Dick and I teamed up and wandered round to see what we could

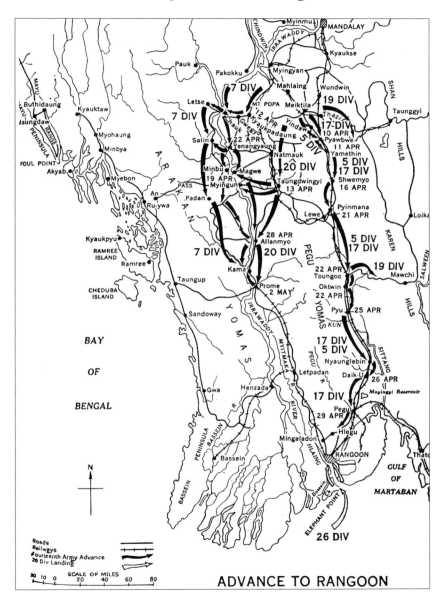

Advance to Rangoon

find by way of souvenirs. I don't suppose we had much ready cash as for a year or so most of us had been sending our pay home as there were so few ways or opportunities to spend money in those parts. We may have had a few Indian rupees but above all we had a commodity which the poor Burmese peasants were glad to acquire – our packets of oatmeal biscuits which had been our 'bread substitute' for many months. I have a clear memory of engaging in a spot of bartering: packets of biscuits for 'genuine Mogok stones', or at least that's what we were meant to believe. We were aware that Mogok, to the north of Burma towards the border with China, had some famous mines which produced precious stones, mainly rubies, but I'm sure we weren't taken in by the sales talk. However, for a couple of packets of biscuits, I acquired three stones of varied colours as souvenirs of my visit to Mandalay. Coloured glass I suspect although I have never troubled to check them out and have lost two of them over the years.

My other memory is of the magnificent Fort Dufferin which was built by the British in the nineteenth century. The 19th Division had to bring up its heaviest guns to breach the thirty-foot walls and then to get across a deep and wide moat before it could drive out the Jap garrison. However Dick and I got into the Fort easily enough, and he reminds me that we came across some nuns from a Convent who were looking after a group of children. They were all very emaciated from shortage of food, but it seemed that the Japs had not troubled them in any physical way which in the midst of terror and death was pleasing.

With our break over we were on the move again. The Japanese were retreating as fast as they could in order to regroup after their defeats at Mandalay and Melktila. The 20 Division now had a role to ambush as many of them as possible and to reach their supply depots before they could do anything about it. The records show that about three thousand of them were killed (there were still very few who surrendered) and many guns and other pieces of equipment were captured. We raced ahead at break-neck speed, rarely stopping in any position for more than a day or two. Don reminds me that we were sent to an OP with an Indian Infantry Unit who had a fleet of armoured cars. We were moving so quickly that we went beyond the range of our guns so we wouldn't have been able to help if the Indians ran into trouble. The leading car spotted some Japs and opened up so they got us to stop and be prepared for anything. However, the enemy were in no mood to fight and sped off in a cloud of dust across the plain. It was soon realised that we had over-run a Jap gun and artillery command post as scattered about were maps, wallets, photos and plotting boards. We were warned to watch out for booby traps but I think they had left in such a hurry that this was unlikely. They had managed to find time to put their guns out of action, one with a long barrel now looking like a peeled back banana skin. A little further on, Don remembers that we were on a good tarmac road for a change and making about 40 miles an hour when we were suddenly given the order to halt and through binoculars he was able to see a group of the enemy seemingly round a camp fire, unconcerned and unaware that we were anywhere near. They soon realised our presence, as a bullet whizzed past Don's right ear. We were obviously just running into groups of disorganised stragglers and all they could do was to bring us to a halt with a few stray bullets and mortar shells. We were soon on our way again heading for Prome, which was the immediate objective for 20 Division. 17 Division were also pushing hard on a parallel track to ourselves, heading for the important town of Pegu. This country was good for the armour and, on one occasion, tanks advanced so fast that in one town a Jap military policeman was found directing traffic when the British tanks appeared. He soon lost his job – and his life.

I can't say that the recollections of Dick Williams and Don Turner always coincide with mine but then we weren't always teamed together for OPs. Here are some of Don's own memories which give a further flavour to the life of an artillery OP signaller during this period of the race for Rangoon.

I remember a night where the OP party were with a Company of Gurkhas whose objective was to block the road across which the Japs would be retreating to the east. We trekked across open country, 'pialas' muffled, arriving at a ditch on the edge of the road and digging in to await the enemy. After a while the order was given to prepare to go in with the bayonet. It seemed a long and cold night although it passed without incident. It was always reassuring to be with the Gurkhas and I was also fortified that night by scoffing an emergency ration of hard chocolate which had been issued on the troopship *Otranto* many months before. The dawn came up early and across the road a Burmese housewife was going about her chores from her little house perched on stilts, unaware that on that day she was at the point of the meeting of the ways of two armies. We moved into a village where a Red Cross Ambulance was parked and I was saddened to see Burmese civilian casualties brought in for treatment. One wounded young woman was carried on a litter, and immediately treated by the doctor. The wounds, I'm afraid, were the result of harassing artillery fire on their village through which the Japs might pass in their retreat. The headman had a collection of 'gems' in his dhoti and I gave him some rupees for a green stone which I later had mounted in a ring for Jean my wife. On our way back we passed a burning ammunition dump. Sadly, two Gurkhas had been killed in dealing with it.

By 1 May both Prome and Pegu had been taken but monsoon clouds were gathering. About the same time landings by sea and air were being made at Rangoon. The invaders found that the Japs had left the city in a hurry and there was great rejoicing as the prisoners of war in Rangoon jail painted a message on the roof for the benefit of reconnaissance pilots – 'JAPS GONE'.

We were soon to go too, much to our surprise and pleasure. The 9th Field Regiment was to be taken out of the 20th Division and returned to India. I suppose there was also some sadness in receiving the news as we would be leaving all those gallant Infantry boys we had shared our lives with from the days of Witok, Moreh, Shenam, Imphal, Ukhrul and so on. They came from Cumbrian towns and villages like Carlisle, Wigton, Silloth, Whitehaven and Workington and from small towns across the Scottish border, Gretna, Lockerbie and Galashiels, all of them familiar names from my childhood and youth in Carlisle. They also came from the heart of England around Northampton and the far south from the hamlets of Devon. Entwined with all these names came also Gurkhas from remote Nepal

THE
TWENTIETH
INDIAN
DIVISION

Farewell Message from The Divisional Commander,

Major-General D. D. GRACEY, C.B., C.B.E., M.C.

to All Ranks of

The Ninth Field Regiment, Royal Artillery.

"Thanks to the grand fighting qualities of our infantry and the magnificent support given by our gunners to them, no tactical disaster has befallen 20th Indian Division since it started to fight the Japs in October 1943. Now a major tragedy has taken place—the transfer of Ninth Field to India out of the Division.

This is as big a blow to me personally as it is to all units in the Division.

I told you all personally after the end of the battle of MANIPUR how much we all appreciated your grand support and fine spirit. In the battles of MANDALAY and IRRAWADDY, you have again given of your best, and we can ask for no better than the best of 'Ninth Field'. Most of you will be going Home soon, and you thoroughly deserve to go. You can go with the satisfaction in your hearts of a job very well done, and with the thanks and gratitude of your British, Gurkha, and Indian comrades at arms of 20th Division and for a short time of 23rd Division, who have been so proud of you always.

I wish you all God-speed, a happy home coming and a prosperous future.

D. D. Gracey

Major-General,
Commander, 20th Indian Division."

SEAC

THE SERVICES NEWSPAPER OF
SOUTH EAST ASIA COMMAND

No. 481   One Anna.

FRIDAY, 4 MAY, 1945.

Printed by Courtesy of
THE STATESMAN in Calcutta.

OUR MEN ENTER RANGOON

KANDY, Thurs.—Troops of the Allied Land Forces entered Rangoon this morning says a special SE Asia Command communiqué.

An APA message says that Allied prisoners released from internment camps on the way to Rangoon say that the Japanese began evacuating Rangoon three weeks ago, by sea and land.

Airmen flying low over the city saw a sign on one Burma building saying: "Japs gone." The sign was framed out of strips of cloth.

Other airmen report seeing about 1,000 men whom they believed to be Allied prisoners. They were in a camp on the west bank of the river opposite Rangoon. They were dressed in khaki-coloured clothes and waved white flags with red strips.

No AA Fire

The past two days have indicated that only pockets of fighting Japanese are left. Airmen have reported no A-A fire over Rangoon for several days.

There is little news yet of the operations at the mouth of the Rangoon estuary, where paratroopers and amphibious forces were landed. Airmen say the gun positions on both banks of the estuary appear largely deserted.

A Press Note says that rocket and cannon-firing Hurr.-straiers of Eastern Air Command are taking a big toll of Japanese transport and materials as the enemy tries to remove accumulated stocks from Rangoon.

Pegu Captured

Never in 221 Group's support of the 14th Army in its drive on Rangoon, has enemy transport been seen in such quantity, but the swift advance had compelled the Japanese to move vehicles and supplies by daylight. Without air cover, and in country ideal for low-level strafing, the enemy has had to rely for protection on small-arms fire, which has done little to interfere with low-level dawn-to-dusk attacks

BERLIN FALLS: HITLER COMMITTED SUICIDE

FLASH FLASH FLASH FLASH

MOSCOW 2/5:— BERLIN IS COMPLETELY CAPTURED. MARSHAL STALIN ANNOUNCED.

REUTER 3/5 BBS/SUSIL 2-54 AM

How the tape machine recorded the end in Berlin

MOSCOW, Thurs.—The fall of Berlin, capture of more than 70,000 prisoners and the news that Hitler and Goebbels committed suicide in Berlin are announced in an Order of the Day issued by Marshal Stalin yesterday.

The Order addressed to troops of the Red Army and the Red Navy said: " Troops of the First White Russian Front, commanded by Marshal Zhukov, in co-operation with troops of the First Ukrainian Front, commanded by Marshal Koniev, today, after stubborn street battle, completed the rout of the Berlin garrison and captured the city of Berlin.

"The garrison of Berlin defending the city, headed by the Officer in Command of the Defence of Berlin and General of the Artillery Webling and his staff, today at 15.00 hours ceased resistance and laid down their arms and surrendered.

"On 2 May, by 21.00 hours, our troops in Berlin took more than 70,000 prisoners."

The Order adds that Red Army troops completed the destruction of the German grouping, surrounded SE of Berlin and between 24 April and 2 May killed 60,000 Germans and took more than 120,000 prisoners.

Goebbels Dead, Too

PEACE COUNT DENIES ALL

LONDON. Wed.—In Stockholm yesterday Count Bernadotte so-called German "surrender envoy" stated at a press conference "I have not seen Himmler during my last visit to Germany and Denmark. I have not forwarded any message from Himmler or other authoritative German to the Allies."

Prime Minister Churchill told the House of Commons yesterday that he will broadcast the news of victory on the Western Front, and will inform the House. The King will broadcast to the

A day to remember, 4 May 1945. The headlines in the SEAC newspaper tell their own story.

and Punjabis and Sikhs from the north-west of India. Our Divisional Commander gave us all a personally signed copy of his farewell message to the Regiment. It was a fitting and very welcome conclusion to a couple of years out of our young lives. We soon collected our meagre possessions to board a Dakota from a small airfield at Tharrawaddy to be taken to Chittagong on the Indian east coast to entrain for pastures new.

Frank Owen, the editor of the South East Asia Command newspaper, considered that the reconquest of Burma by the 14th Army was 'a great feat never before accomplished in history and one worthy to rank with the most splendid military achievements'. As it happened, Rangoon was captured on 3 May 1945, one day before the surrender of German forces to Montgomery on Lüneberg Heath. All the publicity therefore was centred on Europe and the tag 'The Forgotten Army' has remained until this day.

CHAPTER 17

Farewell to 20 Division and back to India

T HE DAKOTA WAS THE WORK HORSE of the US Air Force and was used mainly for supplies, but the discomfort of squatting fully laden on its fuselage didn't bother us one bit. Soon we were gathering around the windows to watch the Burmese paddy fields receding into the distance. The flight was about two hundred miles along the coast of the Bay of Bengal and over the Arakan where the 14th Army first realised that the Jap was not the superman that legend had made him out to be. We slept well that night in relative civilisation, in a building of bricks and mortar instead of canvas, straw or under the canopy of heaven. The next day we learned that our small group was an advance party and had a long journey ahead of us to the Punjab in the north-west of India about a thousand miles away. We were lucky, as most of the Regiment with the guns and 3-tonners had a torrid time hanging about the port at Rangoon for most of July waiting for a ship to take them to Madras. They eventually embarked on the SS *Dunera* on 29 July.

I don't remember that Chittagong (which later ended up in Bangladesh) had much to offer us except a good rest and regular meals. A few of us had some tit-bits which the Quartermaster handed out before we left Burma. Don tells me that he had a 7 lb tin of boned chicken which we all tucked into to celebrate. We were soon to be reminded of the joys of Indian railways, built largely by the British, of course. Our first stop would be Delhi, a journey of about three days and nights in those days. A romantic journey I suppose, across long bridges spanning mighty rivers like the Ganges and the Brahmaputra, through towns and cities like

Patna, Benares, Allahabad and around Agra, although I don't remember a stop to see the Taj Mahal. We would occasionally stop at one of the stations *en route*. From what I have seen on TV, Indian railway stations don't seem to have changed much since those days: many hundreds milling about on the platform selling tea, chapattis and sweetmeats of all kinds; also the odd snake charmer or dancing bear handler. Then if you passed through at dusk or dawn, there would be a sea of white dhotis on the platform, slight figures inside them taking their rest until the next day's round of trading.

At New Delhi we were to pick up transport to take us by road to Dehra Dun about 130 miles north, but we were able to squeeze a few hours break for a look at Old Delhi, a seventeenth century walled city with city gates, narrow alleys and the impressive Red Fort. However, we were soon on our way to Dehra Dun, which turned out to be a very pleasant place in a forest area and on a plateau about two thousand feet above the sticky plain. We were billeted in some of the buildings of the Indian Military Academy which had good living quarters and excellent sports facilities. The various Regiments in the area were soon searching out the best footballers to represent them and great rivalry ensued. The 9th Field Regiment had a good team and got a lot of noisy support from our Battery gunners and signallers, as Dick Williams had been spotted as a steady full back (a term no longer in use in modern soccer). He didn't make the Area team for the big game some months later when Northern Command organised a visit by Tommy Walker's eleven which included a number of famous players of the time – Ditchburn, the Spurs and England goalkeeper; Morris and Robinson of Manchester United; Allen of Wolves; and Rutherford of Glasgow Rangers. There was plenty of scope for us to go wild as nearly half the team were from our Regiment, but in spite of all the support, my well preserved souvenir programme tells me that the visitors won 4–nil.

In July 1945 when we arrived in Dehra Dun our minds were still occupied by the little matter of defeating the Japanese, and it was rumoured that we would be taking part in the next stage before

The final ignominy – under the watchful eyes of Indian soldiers, Japanese officers surrender their swords

the invasion of Japan itself, a landing on the coast of Malaya. For a few weeks we lived under this cloud and the Regiment appeared to be preparing for such an eventuality. The Japanese would be likely to defend their homeland to the last man and we had no illusions about the likelihood of very large casualties if Japan itself had to be invaded. President Truman had other ideas, and the atomic bombs dropped on Hiroshima and Nagasaki on 6 and 9 August soon brought about the unconditional surrender of all the Japanese forces. What a relief. It is understandable that there are many conflicting views about President Truman's decision to drop the bombs. All I can say is that many millions of Allied lives would have been lost in an invasion of Japan and many in the 9th Field Regiment could have been among them.

So 15 August 1945 became to be known as VJ Day, the 50th Anniversary of which has just been celebrated as I write. My memory of the celebrations on the actual day is blurred, except that a 21-gun Victory salute was called for and we duly obliged with great pleasure.

For a number of weeks after VJ Day everything was in a state of flux. Some of those who had enlisted early in the war were going home, and young soldiers were arriving to replace them, but for Burma veterans the organisation of a long leave was a priority. Dick and I chose to have a month in the hill station of Mussoorie in the

After Burma, Norman and Dick on leave in Mussoorie

foot hills of the Himalayas. Hill stations like this one, also Simla and Darjeeling further along the range, were used extensively by the British families for their retreats when it became too hot on the plains. Mussoorie, at about 5,000 ft above Dehra Dun, was ideal for a time of peace with good food and opportunity for leisurely walking in the hills. The views were breathtaking. On a clear day the snow-covered high peaks of the mountains could be seen, Nanda Devi, 25,649ft., being the nearest.

Coming back down the winding road to Dehra Dun and to reality, I found that the CO was keen to see that the reinforcements soon learned the ways of the Battery and yours truly had a part to play as far as the signallers were concerned. With one stripe and another one soon afterwards, I found myself in charge of the F Troop signallers. It was just as well to be busy to avoid fretting over the slow process of repatriation to the UK. It seemed likely that I would still be in India well into 1946. One or two courses were on offer and I was accepted for a three-week course at the RAF Instructors' School at Saharanpur. Out of the ninety or so on the course only nine of us were from the Army, the first course that soldiers had been allowed to join. I see from my letter of 24 October 1945 that I told my parents, 'The course should give me an idea if I'll be any good at school teaching when I'm demobbed.' As I later decided not to pursue a teaching career, I can only conclude that my experience at Saharanpur influenced me in my decision. However, when I got back to the Regiment I had a spell as Signals Instructor at RHQ so I must have coped fairly well. Dick Williams was sure that he wanted to join the Police Force on his demob, so he was pleased to be accepted for the Corps of Military Police and went off to Rawalpindi for training. I felt that being a 'Red Cap' would suit him but to be accepted he had to sign on as a regular for a couple of years. After training he was posted to Africa to try to keep the frustrated soldiery out of mischief in towns like Benghazi and Tobruk. I suspect he would have a livelier time there than when he began plodding the lanes of Cornwall as a Police Constable two years later.

Over the next few months in this settled situation it seems from my letters that life was very pleasant although it was irritating having to watch groups go off to the boat every week. There was a good WVS canteen in the town with ENSA concerts laid on and then there was a regular Sunday Service in the Camp which put me in touch with other Christians including a number of Salvationists. After Christmas, quite a crowd of us from many denominations got together on a week night in what was called the Brigade Chapel where there was an organ. Then on a Sunday night we were introduced to an American Presbyterian Church in the town, and Don and I regularly joined about fifteen others from the camp for the evening service followed by a slap-up supper at the home of a Miss Phillips. No one was in a hurry to get back to the barracks so for an hour or so we had songs round the piano and I was usually roped in to tinkle the ivories.

On reflection, we were 'living the life of Riley' in Dehra Dun and should have appreciated it more, but most of my letters dwelt on how I had to say cheerio to pals who were on their way and my own wish that it was my turn.

Greeting the new arrivals mainly from the British Liberation Army in Europe provided a lot of interest for us. I wrote home at the time that 'I heard quite a few who had been in France saying that they were glad to have been there in preference to Burma, and that as the war was nearing its end in Europe, BLA was often referred to as Burma Looms Ahead.' About that time the film *Burma Victory* was being shown to us, and there was also an American film, *Objective Burma*, in circulation. I wrote in my letter that it was later banned from showing in British cinemas, probably because of the erroneous impression it gave that it was largely the Americans who had re-taken Burma. I said that it was entirely fiction, unlike the British version which had a ring of truth about it. After fifty years I can't confirm the truth of that ban, but I've watched both films recently on video tape and agree with my sentiments at the time. *Burma Victory* is a serious documentary and worth seeing by those wishing to learn about the conditions in that theatre of war. *Objective Burma* was in fact shown recently on TV Channel 4 and the viewing guide said this about it:

> Despite its careless suggestion that Errol Flynn was single-handedly winning the mainly British Burma campaign this is one of the most savagely impressive of Hollywood war films. Flynn leads his paratroopers deep into the jungle to destroy a Japanese radar station and the terrible cost of the mission is never shirked. War correspondent Henry Hull goes crazy with rage (wipe 'em off the face of the earth!); Flynn pulls out a grenade pin with his teeth; and soldier George Tobias says he'll follow him down the barrel of a cannon. Gripping stuff.

You can understand that I switched the TV off halfway through this film, but I still keep my video tape of *Burma Victory* as well as a tape from the 'World at War' series entitled 'It's a lovely day tomorrow' which gives a broader view of the Burma campaign from the retreat through Burma to the Indian border at Imphal.

Surprise, surprise, I wasn't to see my time out at Dehra Dun.

There was the little matter of an expedition to the North West Frontier, an area glamorised in many of the stories of the British Raj. Again the 9th Field Regiment had to pack up its by now considerable stores and be on the move again even if for me it would be only for two or three months.

CHAPTER 18

To the
North West Frontier and home

ON 11 MARCH 1946, I wrote to my parents saying I had just arrived in Nowshera after a week of travelling. Apparently, to reach the so called main road north to the North West Frontier we had first to go south to Delhi where we pitched tents in the grounds of the Red Fort. I wrote:

> the day was Tuesday and INA Victory Week had just started. On Thursday I believe the big parade was interrupted by members of the Congress Party and as a result three people were killed and fifteen or so injured.

(Does anything change!!)

A five hundred mile trip through the plains of the Punjab would be very attractive to many seasoned travellers in the nineties, but to most of us just longing to get home, it was probably a chore. However, my letter recounts the route through Ambala, Jullunder, Lahore, Jhelum and Rawalpindi. The plains were hot and dusty. When our trucks stopped we were besieged by monkeys, but the last lap to Nowshera I describe as

> most pleasant – the great River Indus has its source in the mountains a few hundred miles up in the Himalayas and it has to be crossed to reach Nowshera. A quite marvellous bridge (the Attock) spans it, a combination of road and rail, the latter being above the road. On each side of the Indus the road rises and gives us a grand view as it winds its way to the sea many hundreds of miles away.

My next letter described the amenities at the Regimental Institute where we were to be housed.

The approach to the Khyber Pass, India to Afghanistan, near Nowshera, 1946

It has a separate section for NCOs and is quite well rigged out for comfort. There are billiards and table tennis tables, grassed areas for football, hockey and cricket also a fair menu in the canteen, eggs and chips being the most common meal in the evening. The YMCA and TocH are only a few minutes walk from the billets which are good: brick buildings with electric lights and fans for everybody; the roofs are extraordinarily high which makes for coolness apart from being ideal for indoor badminton. Trips are going to be organised for us to pay a visit to the Khyber Pass which is about thirty miles away. Pleased you have had a few bananas after so long without. Yes, Indian fruit-wallahs come round every day with bananas, oranges, nuts and dates. Things like that are very common for us.

Reading this letter now, it sounds like a holiday camp. With conditions such as these, I expect the regulars of pre-war days couldn't complain at a posting to the North West Frontier even if they did have to contend with a few awkward tribesmen in the Khyber Pass. As it happened, we also had a bit of trouble with the tribesmen. I wrote:

There is a North West Frontier ribbon for this area which is given if we are ever turned out to fire on any hostile tribesmen for a period of twenty-four hours. Of course nobody's anxious to do that, although even round here if we lay any cable and leave it out overnight, half of it has gone the next morning. So the Pathans cause us the extra work of reeling-in after every day's stunt.

Both of my closest pals from Burma days had gone by now. Don had actually managed a month's leave in the UK by plane and boat so I wasn't to meet him again until 'civvy street'. He wrote me two letters from his parents' home in London to give me a taste of what it was like back home. He mentioned the food rationing and the need for clothing coupons saying that 'the girls usually enquire if I have any clothing coupons and always seem interested in stockings (fully fashioned).' His advice to me was, 'If you want to make an immediate hit with the fair sex, just fill up your kit bag and you won't go wrong.' I'm afraid that Nowshera wasn't the place for silk stockings, so any room in my kit-bag was stuffed with shoes, shirts and silk pyjamas for my mother, which I'm sure she would never wear. Another of Don's tit-bits from home referred to the varied comments from friends about his appearance. Some said, 'You haven't changed at all,' others, 'He looks much older,' and again, 'He's quite a man now – of course it's the moustache.' Surprisingly, Don said, he was never asked the stock question which irritated most servicemen on leave: 'When are you going back?' Wearing his bush hat meant that he was considered to be a New Zealander or Australian, which shows the ignorance at home of the Burma campaign and the 14th Army. Burma was a long way off and inaccessible, the war reporters were few and Europe occupied the headlines. Entertainers were thin on the ground too, although Vera Lynn did us proud. Don't forget that getting to the other side of the world was difficult in those days. There were no comfortable jets as there are now, and Vera was one of the few well known artists who was prepared to make the journey to Burma. Not only that, she readily went by jeep or light plane to reach isolated groups of men in the jungle. She was rightly honoured with the MBE.

I seem cheerful enough. I must be going home soon

The Regimental Institute in Nowshera, although very civilised after Burma, was no holiday camp for us. The CO started extensive training to initiate the new intake into our ways. It may have been peace time but it was obviously taken very seriously. My letter of 22 March 1945 says:

Tomorrow I move to Battery HQ to take over in charge of the Battery signals. The situation which has arisen isn't particularly congenial. On Wednesday, the communications out on the scheme to say the least did not go well and seeing that the CO and a few more 'bigwigs' were there, someone had to 'take the can back', so the NCO in charge of signals was up before the Colonel. He was given what is called a 'severe reprimand' and that was that. Anyway, afterwards the Battery Commander decided to take him off the job and make me his successor. The nasty bit is that for the time being he is to remain in the same Troop and he will have the humiliation no doubt of having me there now in charge. The usual thing, if something like that happens, is to post the unlucky chap out of the Troop and often the Battery, but our present BC hasn't a lot of feeling, so there it is.

Within a fortnight another stripe came along. I paid my weekly fee of 5 rupees and became a member of the Sergeants' Mess, which, because of the long tradition of the Raj in Nowshera, was 'well appointed'. We sat down to a three-course meal twice a day served by Indian bearers. You might have thought with all this treatment I would have been looking to sign on for a few years like Dick, but my letters to my parents were still full of the rumours of speedy repatriation and speculation about catching the boat. On 30 April 1946, I was able to tell them:

> The great day has arrived at last. The 9th Field Regiment is left behind for good. At present I am in Rawalpindi where I am staying for a few hours to see my pal Dick and then catching the train for Deolali.'

Four days later I wrote:

> Here I am at the Homeward Bound Trooping Depot, Deolali; what memories are conjured up: my first night in India wondering where we would be posted to. The chaps arriving now get a much better welcome than we got. Still that's all finished with, the important fact is that I'm here this time waiting for the boat.

I had to wait about two weeks to board RMS *Alcantara* at Bombay for a trip very different from the one round the Cape about three years before. No destroyer escort, fully lit up and port-holes open. We sailed across the Arabian Sea and up the Red Sea to Port Said, when after dinner most of us sought to book a bed space on deck. I never liked the hammocks and lying there under the stars, the sea like a mill pond, was the heaven we had imagined back in the hell of Burma. All too soon we were through the Straits of Gibraltar and glad to put away our tropical kit and search for the serge battledress somewhere in the depths of our kit bags. We could tell from the pitching and rolling that we were in the Bay of Biscay and Southampton would soon loom up out of the mist.

CHAPTER 19

Awaiting demob –
filling in with a bit of acting

IT IS DIFFICULT TO DESCRIBE HOW I FELT on my return home after three years abroad, especially when I'm trying to do it after a space of fifty years. It was June 1946 but it hardly felt like summer. The European war had been over for a year. To the surprise of many commentators, Winston Churchill and the Conservatives had been defeated in the first post-war election. The legacy of war was very noticeable, shortages of many items and food and clothes rationing still continuing. In the cities, bomb damage was everywhere. However there was optimism in the air and a determination amongst the British people to get on with their lives. It was now just one of those things when Bill, Jack or Jill arrived home next door resplendent in their demob suits or dresses. The days of greeting 'the conquering heroes' with street parties were over and ex-servicemen and women had to do their best to slip in to Civvy Street again, hopefully to their old job, almost as if the last five years had not changed them or indeed anything else. County cricket was getting under way and stars like Denis Compton and Bill Edrich were resuming their run-making at Lords. Len Hutton was back for Yorkshire and his arm, which had been broken like mine at the humerus bone, didn't seem to be restricting his flow of runs. Hedley Verity was being missed in the Yorkshire and England sides, having been killed in Italy. In Australia, Don Bradman was about to renew his attack on English bowlers. Don Turner, who was still out in India, had a go at summing up his feelings in a letter to me shortly after my return. He wrote:

Well how are you enjoying yourself? I always think of this returning to blighty business as stepping from one existence to another. When out here, blighty seems so far away, and yet, on returning after leave, India and all its peculiarities seemed just as remote. With me there was no question of getting used to it; at times it seemed incredible that I had been away for over two years.

Back in Nowshera the lads were suffering a heat wave; 127°F, Don said, and the Medical Officer had ordered that salt water drinking parades be held twice a day. The heat hadn't stopped them going out on exercises and unfortunately a gun squad had crashed over a bridge near Attock injuring most of the gun crew and killing one of them. I was reminded of the sad happening when we were out on an exercise not long after VJ day, when one of our shell cartridges was faulty and a 25-pounder shell fell short of the target among some poor Infantrymen: a real tragedy, when you consider that many of them had survived Japanese shells for three years.

As I have implied, my homecoming was quiet and strange. My parents had left the shop premises and moved to one of the Carlisle suburbs. I could see in their faces that they had found the last few years very difficult. It is often said that it is a greater strain on the families who are left behind to worry about their loved ones at the front. Of course they had the added pressure of food coupons and the problem of seeing that all their registered customers were treated fairly. No under the counter sausages like Corporal Jones in Dad's Army! I was unsettled because I still couldn't see the end of my time in the Army. Demobilisation seemed to be painfully slow although one couldn't argue with the principle of 'first in, first out'. I had to make the best of it. Soon I was back at the Royal Artillery Depot in Woolwich which was good as I was able to pick up some of the friendships I had made at the Salvation Army there and assume some 'lip exercises' in the cornet section of the Citadel Band. I was badly out of practice.

Formal guard duties on the huge parade ground at Woolwich barracks were still a part of life there, although it was a change as a guard commander to be confined to the guard room instead of doing the two hour patrol duty along one side of the square. As

August arrived we were staggered but rather pleased to see on orders that a couple of hundred of us were to be taken to Fort William to be extras in a film. I should think that the powers that be were very glad to part with us for a few weeks, as they had a problem knowing how to keep us occupied. So in a long column we marched down to the station to catch a night train to Scotland.

The film was *Bonnie Prince Charlie* with David Niven as the Prince and Margaret Leighton as Flora Macdonald. Other main players were well known names at the time – Jack Hawkins, Finlay Currie and John Laurie. A couple of days later the *Daily Mirror* produced a bold headline – 'SOLDIERS ACTING UNPAID'. Our acting amounted to standing around on the slopes of Ben Nevis dressed either as wild Highland Scots in kilts, wielding swords and shields or in the bright red uniform of the English with long barrelled muskets at the ready. I was one of the Scots which proved to be the better bet as many of the English had to hang about in the loch to be ready for shooting (the film of course). The Scots also spent a lot of the time in some kind of formation on the hillsides waiting for the sun to come out from behind the clouds. On the call 'Action' we were expected in double quick time to be in position for the cameras to whirl. The action would often be short lived as the sun wasn't often very obliging. The amateur entertainers and the card sharps amongst us came into their own, as something had to be done to eliminate the boredom.

My experience during this fortnight with rain, cloud, mist and, I must say, little sun, put me off Scottish holidays for the rest of my life. Ethel would often say, 'We could go to Scotland this summer,' and my answer would be, 'I would rather go to Bournemouth.' Even though until 1960 we lived within eight miles of Scotland I reckon I won the argument and it was usually one of the south coast resorts until we moved to Essex when France became our favourite. However, Scotland 'came good' in 1990 when we had two weeks with reasonable weather in the area of Fort William and Oban. We had moved to Teesside on retirement in 1983 and this Scottish holiday was about the last we spent caravanning.

As for the film, it was released by British Lion/London Films in

1948, but the critics gave it the 'thumbs down'. Halliwell's *Film Guide* quotes some of their comments: 'The picture is not lacking moments of unconscious levity, what with David Niven rallying his hardy Highlanders to his Standard in a voice hardly large enough to summon a waiter,' and 'Time has made it the film industry's biggest joke.'

The best that can be said of it is the comment about good Highland photography, which is remarkable considering what we suffered from the weather in the Highlands that August. It was a far cry from northern India. Perhaps I was envious of Don who was still writing to me from Nowshera saying things like, 'Outside the sun is beating down on the sandy soil and when the curtains part it's like a breath from hell,' and a few weeks later, 'The weather has improved [he meant it was cooler], still practically no rain, but prickly heat has gone at last.' Like me some months previously, he had demob on his mind. 'Had a medical the other day,' he wrote, 'Another step towards the consummation of Group 45.' He seemed to enjoy Nowshera as I did, and sent me a few snaps to show what he was up to. So whether we were seeing out our time in India or England (apart from Dick who was soldiering on in Africa) the thoughts on waking every day were about our demob group. Mine was number 42 and the day came when at the Military Dispersal Unit in York, I was handed a Soldier's Release Book and a Certificate of Transfer to the Army Reserve. Looking at these documents now, I am surprised to find a section which says, 'The receipt of this man's greatcoat is hereby acknowledged.' Who knows, without this chitty I might not have been allowed a demob suit. However, clad in my suit and in possession of postal drafts to claim war gratuity and post war credits, I caught the train for Carlisle. It was 22 November 1946, and with three months official leave (paid, I expect) I was transferred to the Army Reserve on 23 February 1947, five years and one month from my call up to Preston.

CHAPTER 20

Reflections

WHEN I REFLECT ON THESE FIVE YEARS from eighteen to twenty-three spent in this way, the questions are endless. To start on a personal note. What did they do for me, my family, how were we changed, how did those years shape the future? How was my faith in God affected? Here are a few thoughts.

Looking again at the cutting showing the nineteen who went in the forces from the Carlisle Citadel of the Salvation Army, I can count fifteen who donned their uniform once more and took their place in the Band. I was one of them, and by the grace of God was able to continue my Salvation Army service, not only in the Band, but also in the work for young people. Ethel, who became my wife in 1950, was also involved in children's work as well as singing in the Songster Brigade. These activities continued for more than a decade, until just before we moved to Essex in 1962 with our two boys, when we decided that a particular Church of England (St James') would be more suitable to our spiritual needs. But because of the depth of my roots, I still have a bond with Salvationists when I meet them, and a respect for the work they do for people in the spiritual and social areas of life.

Quite soon after welcoming the returning servicemen and women, the Corps was anxious to find a way of honouring the one who did not return, Sergeant Navigator Hargreaves Johnstone, RAF, who is buried in Bad Muender Cemetery in Northern Germany. A special Memorial Service was therefore held in the Citadel on 16 June 1946. It was particularly poignant as his mother was a widow and Hargreaves her only son. A new cornet was presented to the Band inscribed to his memory, which I was privileged to play for many years. It was handed to me in an emotional little

THE SALVATION ARMY

𝔐𝔢𝔪𝔬𝔯𝔦𝔞𝔩 𝔖𝔢𝔯𝔳𝔦𝔠𝔢

OF

Sergt. Ed. Wm. Hargreaves Johnstone

R.A.F.

(Killed in action—promoted to Glory—January 14th, 1944)

In the
Carlisle Citadel

Sunday,
June 16th, 1946
at 10-45 a.m.

Conducted by Adjutant R. Bamber, C.O.

From early infancy Edward Wm. Hargreaves Johnstone attended the Carlisle Citadel Corps of the Salvation Army. At seven years of age he joined the Young People's Band, and soon became a good Cornet player.

During boyhood, he came to know Jesus as his Saviour, and entered young manhood strong in the Christian faith.

In July, 1942, when eighteen years of age, he joined the R.A.F. and soon rose to the rank of Sergeant Navigator. Wherever he was stationed he linked up with the Salvation Army, witnessing in the meetings and assisting the Musical Sections.

His last night in England was spent at Skegness. He went to the Salvation Army Hall to play a Cornet Solo in a Musical Programme. The members of his bomber crew were present. They were proud of their Salvationist Navigator and were demonstrative in their appreciation of his sterling Salvationism.

The following night his plane was shot down over Germany. He and his American Pilot were laid to rest in the Bad Muender Cemetery, seventeen miles south-west of Hanover.

"They shall not grow old as we that are left grow old.
Age shall not weary them, nor the years condemn,
At the going down of the sun, and in the morning
We shall remember them."

Hargreaves Johnstone gave the last full measure of devotion. He is the only comrade of the Carlisle Citadel Corps to make the Supreme sacrifice in the World War.

ceremony, as the Bandmaster was aware that I had probably been his closest friend.

At the time of the 50th Anniversary celebrations of VE and VJ days, many commentators challenged the sixties and seventies generations by posing the question, 'If you were put to the test, if you were asked to risk your lives over five or six years, or put up with the privations and sacrifices of your elders, would you be able to do it?' (*Daily Mail*, 8 May 1995). The answer given was, 'Who can say? The call to arms has not come, the sacrifices have not been necessary.' Well, surely that's a good reason for celebrating the 50th Anniversary with thanksgiving.

I have already referred to the fact that most of my generation had a basis for their lives gleaned from some Christian training and knowledge, often learned in Sunday School but also from their parents. Based on my service experience, I have a feeling that this training bore fruit in the character of the war-time generation. I am sad that since the war much less attention has been paid to providing the children and young people with that moral and spiritual background which I believe proved so invaluable to me and many others like me during those difficult years.

It is interesting that these two words are included in Section One of the Education Reform Act 1988, which says that the School curriculum 'should promote the spiritual, moral, cultural, mental and physical development of pupils at the school and of society; and prepare pupils for the opportunities, responsibilities and experiences of adult life.' I spent my working life as an Educational Administrator and am now a School Governor, and I know that Head Teachers do their best to promote these aims of spiritual and moral development, but sometimes feel they are losing the battle. Some think it is expecting too much of the school and I have heard them point out that in any week, teachers spend a minimal amount of time with the children compared with the time spent with their parents.

Of course I accept that there were those in Britain with a sharpened liberal conscience who were in a dilemma in 1938/9 as war clouds gathered. In fact, over the last four hundred years many have been tortured in their conscience, as wars have come and gone in that time. In the sixteenth century, Thomas More agreed with his friend Erasmus that there was nothing in the least glorious about war. He tells us that the inhabitants of his ideal state, Utopia, 'hate and detest war as a thing manifestly brutal.' The Utopians went to war cautiously and reluctantly; but go to war they did for a variety of reasons, mainly that war was permissible to protect one's own territory or that of friends against invasion; 'to free some wretched people from tyrannical oppression and servitude'. After the war, one of the dwindling band of Utopians was H.G. Wells. He had lived in London during the war and it is said that in 1946 he was quite depressed. He had really believed for most of his life that with the opportunities for education and travel then available, people would be more understanding and would behave better – they hadn't.

Philosophers and lawyers had agonised over these matters for years, but in the end it seemed to many of them that, for better or for worse, war was an institution which could not be eliminated from the system. All that could be done about it was, so far as possible, to codify its rationale and to civilise its means. This is quite an admission on the frailty and depravity of human nature, about which the Christian message on the redeeming work of Christ Jesus has a lot to say.

During the 50th Anniversary celebrations many of the controversial issues were given a thorough airing in the various media, but it seemed that most commentators concluded that if there was such a thing as a just war, this was it. One wrote, 'that the war was fought to destroy the most odious and dangerous totalitarianism ever to come into existence and to make the world a safer place; it was not fought in vain.' I feel sure that's true.

However, the proclamations of those earlier philosophers may equally have not been in vain, as their thinking probably influenced the great powers to sign what became known as the Geneva Convention which attempted to formulate some rules on the conduct of war, with particular emphasis on the treatment of prisoners. This takes me straight to the Japanese. Their abominable and inhumane treatment of prisoners is now well established, and I thank God I didn't fall into their hands as these memoirs, if written at all, would have been very different. Many of the men who were prisoners on the 'Railway of Death' from Siam (now Thailand) to Burma have been unable to forgive their captors, and having read some of their stories I can well understand their attitude. I must say that if I had had to suffer the beatings, humiliation, starvation and lack of medical treatment, I don't know how I would have felt. In fact, one-third of them didn't survive and many of those who did are still suffering physically and mentally from their ordeal. It was, however, very moving during the 50th Anniversary celebrations to hear the stories of a number who have made a valiant attempt to forgive, in particular the effort made by Eric Lomax (featured in a TV reconstruction), to meet and greet his Japanese principal torturer, both of them now old men. His book *The Railwayman* is a moving testimony and an insight into the minds of the Japanese of that generation: a generation of young men steeped from the day they could talk in militaristic and warlike slogans, naturally leading in the thirties to the inhumane and beastly activities in China and Manchuria, and in the forties to Pearl Harbour, Singapore, Malaya, Burma and in many of the islands of the Pacific.

My generation has lived for over fifty years with the war time memories constantly coming to the surface and many have endured mental torment because of them. Few however have taken the path to peace of mind in the same way as Eric Lomax described in his book:

> From a hundred yards away I saw him walk out on to the bridge over the River Kwai. He could not see me. It was important to have this last momentary advantage over him; it prepared me, even now that I no longer wanted to hurt him. I had forgotten how small he was, a tiny man in an elegant straw hat, loose kimono-like jacket and trousers. From a distance he resembled an oriental carving, some benign wizened demon come to life. Once he had been my interrogator, the mouthpiece of my torturers. I remember him saying to me again and again, 'Lomax you will tell us,' in a voice I hated so much.
> He began a formal bow, his face working and agitated, the small

figure barely reaching my shoulder. I stepped forward, took his hand and said in Japanese, 'Good morning, Mr Nagase, how are you?' He looked at me; he was trembling, in tears, saying over and over: 'I am very, very sorry . . .' I led him out of the terrible heat to a bench in the shade; I was confronting him. At that moment the very capacity for reserve and self control that had seen me through the horror of the Japanese war camp helped me to help him, murmuring reassurances as we sat down.

He said to me: 'Fifty years is a long time, but for me it is a time of suffering. I never forgot you.' He looked deep into my eyes when he said this. His own face still looked like the one I remembered, rather fine-featured with dark and slightly hidden eyes.

Then he asked if he could touch my hand. I didn't find it embarrassing. He gripped my wrist with both his hands and told me that when I was being tortured – he used the word – he measured my pulse. His grief seemed far more acute than mine. 'I was a member of the Imperial Japanese Army; we treated your countrymen very, very badly,' he said. 'We both survived,' I said encouragingly, really believing it.

This incident surely confirms that God's spirit is at work in the heart of His creatures, and if it is heeded can bring good out of evil. Some years ago a Burma Campaign Fellowship Group was formed who 'believe that something of value in Anglo-Japanese relations can be achieved by promoting understanding between those who once fought against each other.' A number of former POWs are members of this group. Bishop Leonard Wilson comes to mind again. Referring to the Japanese military policeman who had taken part in his torturing four years earlier, the Bishop said that 'he had seldom seen so great a change in a man. He looked gentle and peaceful, even though he was going back to serve a ten-year sentence.' The Bishop later administered communion to him in the prison.

In 1995, the Japanese Prime Minister went as far as he could to make a public apology, on behalf of the nation, for atrocities committed in its name, although there are still many former prisoners who don't think his words went far enough and who are pressing for compensation.

The dropping of the atomic bombs has caused much heart searching and I have already said that without them the 9th Field Regiment could have been involved in the invasion of Malaya and Japan. The bombs may have saved my life, and millions more on both sides, so what more can I say? The views of the historians divide on whether or not the Japanese would have surrendered if the bombs had not been dropped. But I understand that at least two of the six key advisers directing their war machine were strongly against surrender, and three days after the dropping of the second bomb they were still urging the nation to fight on. The Army Chief of Staff pointed out that the soldiers were not permitted to surrender, because the nation's military penal code had severe penalties for anyone who laid down their arms. For him there was only one honourable alternative to surrender – suicide. Akira Fujiwara, then a young battalion commander, but now a professor of history, wrote in a book which was critical of his country's war-time conduct, 'I was preparing to die, surrender could occur only in the wake of extraordinary events' – which is precisely what happened when the atomic bombs fell.

A number of Burma veterans have written their memoirs and amongst those I have read I believe I can detect a common thread. It is as if the climate, the hardships, the enemy and the consciousness of being many thousands of miles from home in very alien surroundings conspired to bring out the best in them. It was as though they were aware that they were confronted here with a supreme test, and that qualities which they were unaware of were being drawn out of them: qualities of the spirit, of selflessness, courage and determination. Many of their stories are more impressive than mine; for instance that of Philip Stibbe who, as a Chindit, was badly wounded and eventually captured and tortured. To me it is amazing that he could say after it was all over that 'along with a deep feeling of thankfulness there is a conviction that it was all supremely worth while'. Others have said that they wouldn't have missed it for the world. I can echo similar sentiments. Without doubt my life has since been coloured by the experiences during those five years in the Army but particularly the time spent in

Burma. Who knows what different attitudes to life I might have had if these experiences had not come my way?

So my two flags hang together and for those serving under them it could be said that allegiance to a cause and endurance under difficulties are common to both. St Paul often used the language of warfare in his letters to early Christians and in one of them he exhorted his young friend Timothy to "endure hardship as a good soldier of Jesus Christ". For Salvationists and for all Christians the war goes on and as a last word on the subject I can think of nothing better than St Paul's words to the Ephesians:

> Our struggle is not against flesh and blood, but against the rulers, authorities and powers of this dark world and against the spiritual forces of evil in the heavenly realms. Therefore put on the whole armour of God so that when the day of evil comes you may be able to stand your ground, and after you have done everything, to stand.

Postscript

It is a sad thought for veterans that Burma (now called Myanmar) has had a tempestous fifty years since independence. Aung San Suukyi, a Nobel Peace Prize winner (and even third in the BBC 'Today' programme's poll for Personality of the Year), is now well known throughout the world for her remarkable courage and devotion to her cause. The Party she founded, the National League for Democracy, won the election of 1989 but the Generals refused to hand over power and she was placed under house arrest; her movements are still very restricted. After the war her father had signed an agreement with Prime Minister Attlee which promised the election of a Constituent Assembly and independence, but he did not live to see their implementation – 19 July 1997 is the 50th Anniversary of his assassination.